T0065574

ABC OF
INNER WORLD

ABC OF INNER WORLD

A Philosophic-scientific Perspective

Dr. Swaran J. Omcawr

PARTRIDGE
A Penguin Random House Company

*Disclaimer: The psycho-spiritual suggestions contained in the book
are never intended to replace professional psychological, psychiatric
or medical advice.*

Author can be contacted at:
http://www.speakingtree.in/public/4db961c2
Omcawr Swaran J on Face book
Twitter@Swaran_j
e:mail: jswaran09@gmail.com

To order additional copies of this book, contact
Partridge India
000 800 10062 62
orders.india@partridgepublishing.com

www.partridgepublishing.com/india

Contents

In **ABC of Inner World**, Dr. Swaran J. Omcawr struggles to free spirituality from two extremes; rigid rationalism . . . and our fondness of veneration of conclusions of truth. With unique straightforward approach he endeavors to create a chain of thoughts in reader's mind beginning with raw and simple ones, moving on to more and more intricate and reaching finally at the summit of realization explosion. This may or may not happen in an individual reader; which entirely depends upon how one takes his words— understands or visualizes; engages intellect or subjective awareness for this endeavor! His effort to create the creative insight in readers mind is reinforced with passages on contemporary drift regarding theme of spirituality. While attempting this he takes care not to unnecessarily feed the reader with unwanted information but leads his mind to the pinnacle of subjective awareness. Off and on he calls for leaving the absurd intellectual understanding of this 'pointless universe' and deferring it for a while and come to a bit of realization of one's own subjectivity! He talks about putting phased end to institutionalized construction of intellectual mind which eats away the best years of life. He talks about silently entering into depths of realization that surpasses all understanding!

Dr Swaran J Omcawr (b. 1960), India born author and postgraduate in Human Physiology, is Associate Professor in a Medical College. He is self learned, self guided spiritual enthusiast & generally beseeches holism and eco-consciousness in his lectures.

I dedicate this work to the 'entire neutral universe' which made me think like universe does.

Swaran J. Omcawr

Photography by Chandan Parbhakar

About me . . . .

Deeply embedded in the sea of self where all activities merge into inactivity; swimming in the waters of our universal co-existence; floating over last straw of attachment and flying in the all open skies of liberty . . . . . .

The same thing must we understand now. We are known to this 'freedom' as a word. But look, there may be some better word, having some better meanings, a better engagement of us in the world! There may be some better realization of it. There may be some better theme than this 'liberation'; we may not have known still; nature's deeper design; a deeper gift for us being here in the world. Why do we want to intellectualize it to carry it forward? Schematically and academically!! Why should we again make it obsolete like this much abused word 'freedom'? Let the charm of having it without our 'knowledge' remains!

. . . .

Prophets of yore have left their time. They have given you the basic ideas to comprehend reality. But you cannot put their solutions to your current situations. Now you are the prophet of your life. Now you need to cultivate the prophetic vision.

. . . .

So it is not the question of one soul present in individual body. It is the soul of humanity in all humans or soul of creation in all creation or soul of universe in whole of universe. When you individualize it is the same soul manifesting. The universal soul gets fragmented in finer fragments and is individualized but not personalized. In a group this individuation fades away. When an individual creation dies away it dies fully, it does not leave behind soul. It simply falls short of life. Soul is not personal. Personal elements in us are ego and mind which are born with the body and die with it. There is no universal abode of departed souls. This single fact if understood and realized properly decides our complete liberation after death.

If we clearly apperceive the difference between direct apprehension in whole-mind and relative comprehension by reasoning-mind divided into subject-and-object, all the apparent mysteries will disappear

—WEI WU WEI

Acknowledgements

My sincere most thanks to my daughter Supriya, my son Raikva and their mother Krishna for their understanding and putting faith in me during writing of this book.

I am indebted to Dr. R.S. Sidhu, Additional Professor for his valuable suggestions while preparation of the manuscript.

I am also grateful to Dr. Mridu Grover, Professor for her deep interest in the subject and giving important inputs during discussions.

I am grateful to all others in my life who were silent contributor in their own manner and encouraged in their own way in my journey towards understanding of the subject.

I do acknowledge the contribution of the websites, www. thinkstockphotos.in, www.commons.wikimedia.org/, and www. clker.com for the images which I have used in the book.

I do acknowledge Wikimedia, Internet Encyclopedia of Philosophy, Stanford Encyclopedia of Philosophy and various other websites for their contribution in shaping my thoughts.

Swaran J. Omcawr

How to read this Book
&
How to read life as a whole . . .

. . . . there is a beautiful story; a story regarding the contrast between contemplative state of mind and the tense state which may exist at the same time in a person. This parable quite an ancient one has appeared in certain Indian texts as a story of chronicler of great epic Mahabharata, Rishi Ved Vyasa's son Sukhdeva and King Janaka, a great spiritual seeker and ruler. A more modernized version appeared in Brazilian writer Paulo Coelho' great work "Alchemist". I am narrating the central idea from both. A father sent his young budding son to one highly intelligent & wise man for initiation into spiritual life and to learn some deeper truths of life. After much struggle boy reached his resident place only to see that said wise man was living in a huge mansion more so a palace. By the time boy reached, the wise man was busy with some guests. So he asked young guy to wait. But to make use of the time he proposed that boy should see his palace. As an afterthought wise man added further to take an oil lamp along with but instructed him to take care that no oil should spill from it. The boy obeyed and came back after visiting the palace. The wise man was free now. Boy was eager to have some contemplative talk but wise man asked his impressions regarding the palace. He asked regarding the beautiful interiors, the garden, the flowers, the birds chirping there and whether boy had taken a look in the library and seen some wonderful manuscripts . . . . etc. etc. The boy was bit hesitating and replied that he could not go that far as he had to take care of the lamp. "Then you should go and see the whole palace again, see all the things as whole, both their physical and aesthetic part & get the impression and you'll take care of oil too . . . !" So boy once again saw the most wonderful things in the palace; he appreciated them with his heart and at the same time he concentrated over his body movements and didn't allow his mind to go awry & held back his concentration. The boy found wisdom in synthesis of the uneasy apprehension of keeping balance and yet maintaining the calmness of mind.

. . . . perhaps it is all that we need while moving in life and while reading a good contemplative book too. Our life is a curious mix of ease and tension. Both play their part during natural progression of thought. Reading a book outdoor and without fully calm mind will lead to a hurried opinion. A thought or opinion made during tense state may not be the same thought which we get during ease of contemplation. But to create contemplative mind during stress because of some pressing thought activity one is to become super aware so as the stress don't meddle in the thoughtful meditation.

-Dr. Swaran J. Omcawr

Forward
(. . . to the reader)

Intellectual journey of man was never one-dimensional. Understanding of our true inner nature is said to be the central point of all our scientific researches. Spirituality which means seeking other dimensions of existence caters to this endeavor the most thereby a scientific area of research too. Making it sacred simply is to make us committed to our journey. In spiritual research man is not only a researcher but also the laboratory where he does his research. The search for meaning of our temporal as well as eternal existence shouldn't be left to few intellectual men or saints. Every individual should have the right as well as the longing to know the reality behind his existence. Mother Nature has bestowed us with an intelligent brain and perhaps this is the debt that we should repay back by delving into her secret core.

ABC . . .' was not conceived as a resource book on the subject of spirituality. It is not a compilation of varied material, academic or religious written by many authors on the subject. Reader might have his own intellectual doubts regarding spirituality in life and certain others might be in need of academic exploration of the topic. So at the outset I want to make clear that this not that sort of book. This is rather a book which tells you how to use your own resource that means your mind, your wisdom and intellect to enter into this vast field; and how to leave the intellectual understanding you have amassed since your younger days and enter into the space of stillness. The purpose here is to look for inner creativity and search for insight in the mind. A book becomes insightful only when you make it so. Only need is to enlighten the mind, ignite a creative fire in it and let the mind come out of slumber. Reader is always encouraged by the author to use own mind and to read beyond the words. He is encouraged to do his own investigations before believing anything and encouraged to enter into the mind and fineness of his spirit to find the real truth in his own inner core.

By insight it means a rush of lucid thoughts which give mind a certain clarity and purpose. A single thought from a carefully read book is sufficient to cause this rush. Each one of us is at the different thresholds of the ignition point for the insight. Readers who consume books rather than read them remain burdened with stale thoughts. One and the same thought can be insightful for some and may be entirely naive for others. Difference is one person is busy gathering intellectual thoughts and other has started realizing at his own feeling level. A good reader can find many insightful thoughts from the work of well known or little known authors.

While writing of this book I have avoided lengthy and tiresome discussions on philosophy, theology or any such subject but kept the essence of matter in very simplified and scientific way. One of its aims is to get you out of the prison of mind, understanding & intellectuality. This book is not authored as an intellectual philosophy or some new theory. It is not a philosophy at all religious or otherwise. If you read it as one its terrific aim will be lost. Perhaps that is why I have used sparingly the academic references, known spiritual terms, list of authors or the spiritual authorities and sometimes I simply use a single common term the spiritualists or spiritual persons knowing well that all these traditions of the world has one common basis i.e. man and his relation with his inner and outer world. All previous authors who have done marvelous work on spirituality have discovered uncontested spiritual truths. My idea is to rouse interest of reader in the whole extraordinary field and never to invite blind faith in one particular tradition or religion. And at the same time I have stayed away from providing readers some easy how to do methods on spirituality but relied on expanding the horizon of mind. To rely on methodology is again an intellectual exercise which this book certainly avoids.

We have followed our parents and elders regarding observance of spirituality in our daily life. Following their elders in turn they have almost reduced this vast field of spirituality to mere ritualism. Certain others put it before their children as moral disciplinary code and rely on religious stories to put young minds in rigid moral cage. Such minds lose freedom of thought. We also know that ritualistic practices and disciplinary morality lose a little shine in rational minds. Our generation is either obsessively attached to religion, the ritualistic or decorative side of it or entirely throws it away for some reason or the other. End result is that there is either absolute avoidance of the topic or utter non-belief among our young friends. Atheism is not non-belief. Atheism is a scientific venture. It is rather giving preference to personal efforts to the personal problems and not relying on faith.

But atheist minds sometimes lose faith in their own efforts. Excessively involved with the outer they create a gap in comprehension of their inner world. This gap created in younger days generally culminates into over-enthusiastic religious practices in later life. At that stage they almost altogether lose freedom of the thought. They create for themselves a prison of moral practices or some sort of irrational religious cage. They tend to see every other in same religious moral frame as they see themselves or their children. My idea of bringing this book especially to the young readers is to create temper for thoughtful scientific inquiry; create faith in one's own observations; not only understand but realize their inner world while doing the outer activities. They won't create a spiritual gap when they grow up and become involved in life. They will retain the freedom of observation and thought up to their last days.

This book does not deal much with the outer objective side of religion or God or any such matter of interest, how the people have described or objectified this subject in past. I have spoken very little on these matters. But this book does deal with understanding of Self or *atma,* whatever you call. It deals with other subtle aspects of the reality in a real subjective way by taking the reader to his own inner core. In ancient times all knowledge quests were for this aspect of inner world and people would go to any length to find truth behind their existence. They would leave royal and comfortable life of home and dwell in forests in company of spiritual masters. Spiritual masters won't teach them concluded truths, which they have discovered till date. They would teach them by putting their mind in different thoughtful mode i.e. how to create doubt, investigate it and reach at the truth. At times they would make all the disciples sit near and open up the shell of life like peeling off the layers one by one. That was how the tradition of Upanishads was started during early development of ancient Indian thought. Upanishads are great books but if your mind is trained to feed on conclusions, on quotation work of others you won't feel that charm in reading them. These are charming only to the doubtful.

Down the ages this aspect of finding truth from doubt and investigation has been reduced to over decorative and enthusiastic spiritual practices which usually paint our life black or white in strict good and evil terms. Today people are not doubtful. They know where their God live and what He does and what He demands from us. God is so objectified that you can ask favors through prayers and by offerings. This type of God is God of imagination. On the other side there is advent of many secret or open spiritual societies and groups who claim ascension of soul right up to the abode of God in the higher worlds. Why do they do so, what is the benefit? Is it sheer psychological benefit that we are driving or some real change would occur someday, who would say? All such practices address the needs of the mind not of soul. When totality or wholeness of life has been done away and duality of mind has taken precedence, a part of mind would be fashioned by these practices while rest of mind would be engulfed in the awful darkness. This is the reality of all such societies.

There is commercialization of the real subtlety of spiritual life in the name of saving mankind. Money earning and raising big houses of spirituality, encouraging personality worship and gathering wide followings are star attractions of spiritual quest of these days. And because of penchant of man for enslaving and for power over individuals this theme has been deeply communalized. There is communalization and politicizing of religion reducing the seeker as mere pawn or worthless devotee. This has made unfortunate subjects a tool for getting worldly powers. Collection of hard earned money from these devotees has made these houses extremely powerful and ruthless in their approach. If we have to choose an uncomfortable zone of being alone and finding truth through exploration of one's own self and an easy method of following gurus and guides of society most of us would choose the latter. For mere ease of approach we worship a particular personality or a sect and spend a life time following them without any palpable understanding of the subject. How would we understand reality by following a created model of reality, that too when this model is obsolete and ineffective to our current mental & intellectual temper?

Not only the proclivity of man to be amongst powerful, individual man has not won over his fondness for pleasures, for ease and comforts in life. Hasn't man made himself a heartless consumer for everything available on this planet and by making all our natural resources commercially sellable? Current advances in exploration of other planets are our covert ways to search for quarters where our ever expanding hedonic demands can be met. Of all the biological creation we are among the top for global damage. We have destroyed this globe to meet our comforts. Spirituality for some is another way to seek pleasure and a means to escape reality of life. So spiritual seekers have become consumers and spirituality is now becoming a super-saleable commodity. We even understand that people are doing this for making bucks. But our insecure mind doesn't care. We go to the big spiritual houses with sufficient funds but insufficient home work and end up with much abused field of personality worship and religious slavery. We end up in creating more insecurity in the minds by our frantic search to conquer it.

Our next tragedy is that for mere practice of religion collectively we have become an unmanageable crowd. We have become fanatically religious and violent individuals and act furiously against our own kin having different faith than us. How much do we get detached from reality especially when we observe religion collectively is explained in next example? Here in India people gather in vast numbers at temples and other religious places for joint worship. Certain make shift unprofessional structures are erected around the religious places to accommodate this vast crowd. At times such structures are unable to bear the thrust of the ever rising crowd and give in and people go haywire. Panic strikes and they lose their sense of safety, their faith in the deity and self-management and self control in just one go. Many of the poor fellows lose their life while a good number are injured and almost all of them feel the hell let loose during such stampedes. It is more than unfortunate that these incidences are repeated every year and people won't even bother that this has happened before.

This sort of religious stampede is a manmade tragedy. There is a scriptural wisdom never hidden from dumbest of the dumbest human that the advent of truth in one's mind or the reality or the *kripa* (bless) etc. whatever you call is totally an individual effort and individually obtained and one may obtain it sitting at the corner of one's own house. The collective psyche, crowd, organized worships only give hypnotic angle to our quest and end up in bondage even more rigorous than the worldly bondage. The iron in our soul seeks transformation to become steel and be free of all attachments. But should it be otherwise i.e. to get detached from one magnet of worldly bondage and become attached to another magnet of religious fiefdom?

Spiritual research is not a search for supernaturalism or to validate it. It is not to create more supernaturalism in the form of fallacies in our own natural world. This world is both apparent and hidden to our eyes. We call the hidden world as supernatural. For validating this we have imagined supernatural gods and goddesses and many associated belief based doctrines. Mental imagery sometimes become so strong that passionate devotees may create personified visualization of these gods. But that does not prove their existence in the real world. These doctrines for example those of astrology or worshipping fearful gods or demons and spirits are not only scientifically incorrect but spiritually dishonest too. We must understand that idea of creation of such weird supernaturalism is only a tool for commercial exploitation of spirituality. This is done simply for purpose of creating a spiritual consumerism in the society by creating fear and insecurity. Just look at how spiritual giant Swami Vivekananda blasts the idea of supernaturalism in his major treatise 'Rajayoga'.

> The idea of supernatural beings may rouse
> to a certain extent the power of action in
> man, but it also brings spiritual decay. It
> brings dependence; it brings fear; it brings
> superstition. It degenerates into a horrible

belief in the natural weakness of man. There
is no supernatural, says the *Yogi* . . . .

Dr. Swaran J. Omcawr
Amritsar (India)
May-2014

Prologue

Pure physicality

Pure movement of awareness

Within the body, within the brain, within the mind

No influence—religious or dogmatic

Psychological or spiritual

Scientific or irrational

No pre-professed view of these

Howsoever sacred, howsoever cherished

No guidance, no conclusion

Intense questioning, intense effort

Intense desire to find

Till one is very near to cross the borders . . . !

Till one is very near to the pure intelligence within . . . !

Till one is very near to get the insight!!!

— **0** —

(1)

Advent of new Upanishad

(Let's come closer a bit!)

Biological man is a byproduct of evolution. But his transition from animal, to complete psycho-spiritual entity is partly because of his obsessive pre-occupation with the observer that is he himself. Right from his Neanderthal age infancy to the space age maturity his primary fixation remains to observe and create. His fixation is not only the observance of universe which is external to his senses but also of a universe right within.

On this exploration route he is instrumental for the growth & development of physical world and at the same time of his inner world. His never ending search for unraveling the mysteries of the nature has led to enhancement of his intellectual wisdom superadded by thorough revolution of his psyche. His relentless struggle for expansion of his private territory in the world has led to similar expansion of his inner territory. But unfortunately what is true for one man may not be true for the rest of mankind. And that perhaps is the reason we find different grades of humanity on this planet. On one side if we find men enjoying intellectual freedom of highest order yet there is no dearth of being who are just crossing the biological abyss. Badly conditioned by their desires, food or sex, they would rather love to, as Nietzsche[1] once said, go back to the beasts rather than surpass the man.

Does today's man feel any need to go beyond himself? Has he developed enough mental, intellectual and observational tools for this endeavor? Does it bother him anyway when he finds a compulsive hidden animal in him not at all under his conscious control? Despite enough intellectual wisdom amassed since centuries of self-introspection which could get him some decent humanistic garb why yet he is a slave of psycho-biological compulsions?

Does he forever desire to remain helpless creature in the hands of nature? On one step lower he is age old struggling

---

[1]   **Friedrich Wilhelm Nietzsche a 19**[th] **century** German philosopher, cultural critic, poet and composer. "All creatures hitherto have created something beyond themselves: and do you want to be the ebb of the great tide, and return to the animals rather than overcome man? Man is something that should be overcome. What have you done to overcome him?" he writes in 'Thus Spake Zarathustra', his master treatise.

His fundamental contention was that traditional values had lost their power in the life of individuals. Whole human behavior is motivated by the will to power. In its positive sense, the will to power is not simply power over others, but the power over oneself that is necessary for creativity. Supermen are those who have overcome man i.e. the individual self—and sublimated the will to power into a momentous creativity. Source: http://www.age-of-the-sage. org/philosophy/nietzsche_philosophy.html psychosocial compulsive super animal and on the step next he would be a superhuman with freedom of mind and body with all compulsive emotions in his control! This is assuredly speculated in this century of scientific reason rigorously struggling to find truth in the age old philosophic-spiritual thought. Only demand from man is to stop being animal or triumph the animal within. Another one if added quickly is not to give undue importance for change in 'thinking mind' which alters his behavior superficially without real change in his psyche.

Why man is so helpless to cross this 'rift' of animality? The hidden animal in him is actually driving the human and not other way round. Animal is an automata, the biological machine which runs with biological needs. The cognitive evolution in us has created an 'executive self' and made us in-charge of this machine with shift in consciousness from lower to higher. Ultimate goal of humans is to understand this machine and be at the driving seat and not to let machine remain an automata. Man continuously endeavors to struggle out of this biological predilection to be a human. Start from the basic biological requirements the hunger, the thirst etc. you can move the ladder up to compulsive hidden needs of 'territorial imperative' and still higher his struggle to survive against all competitive odds and exerting superiority over his nearest kin everything is conditioned and with an unconditional surrender to animal. There is cyclical tendency of action and reaction in his entire mental disposition found in his thinking behavior or reactions to the ensuing events of life which unfold as a consequence. This is the vicious cycle of his thought and action that man is unable to do away.

Would the psycho-spiritual guidelines in the contemporary world help him triumph over his crazy animal and frail human? Whether the intellectual caliber achieved because of his enormous struggle down the ages ever become an equivalent of his spiritual up rise or would it mean to be masking his animal with a human makeup? Unless changed evolutionally nothing can be said with certainty, certain thinkers would say. But evolutionary changes are invisible; are there any step up ways which could generate some palpable change in his psycho-physiology which could be termed as spiritual change? Above all what does this term 'real change' actually means?

To find the answers, If we examine closely we would find that we always react to something and never act of our own. The action springs from nature and we merely react. Our reactions are our psycho-social needs of survival. We react as a body to the physical forces of nature or as a psyche to the mental challenges. Every single reaction we make carry similar physical and psychological consequences. Physical ones are seen in our natural world which we continuously strive to make orderly to our needs. Psychological changes are seen when man pursue these reactions endlessly with an ultimate aim of establishing himself as an undisputed ruler of the territory.

We are bound to follow every single reaction we make and then follow reactions of the reaction and create an endless chain of consequences. At a given time we have enough stockpiles of our past and future actions, accomplished or unaccomplished along with series of their consequences on the work table of life. So badly entangled we are in this chain that we have just forgotten the original action from which this whole chain of reactions started. We may not be able to refer to exact situation in our life which was the cause of these endless reactions. We can term this exact point as original action or as pure action. For pure action we mean an action arising in psyche which didn't have any progenitor as its cause. This sort of action definitely was there or had come in our life a long time back and had become the cause of all other consequences. But having forgotten that, we are now programmed enough to respond and carry forward its endless reactions.

Spiritual people are of habit to include actions of previous lives as progenitor of this endless continuous chain. You may theorize endlessly as we find it in Hindu and Buddhist traditions but without any substantial evidence. That perhaps is why in spirituality we have created more faith than reason. All a scientist would say that man is genetically continuing the lives of his forefathers. A past action would be a genetic continuity of actions started by our forefather who left a particular genetic makeup in the offspring's nervous reflexes and that perhaps is why they take up certain actions as genetic continuity. Even on behavioral side our forefathers may have left certain actions unaccomplished which we take up as a family or sociopolitical tradition. For example a defeated ruler gives enough genetic, social and moral inputs to his progeny to reclaim the political as well as psychological territory. These continuing actions are retrieved from our common genetic memory pool putting whole humanity in a karmic bondage since centuries. But all this is rather deviation from our current theme.

The chains of actions and reactions are our mental burden we must be freed from. To complete a single important action in our life we have created so many subsidiary actions that freedom looks a distant dream. It certainly takes more than a lifetime deal to tackle them one by one. While doing so we will create many secondary actions which have potential to create their own chain. The original chain and supplementary chains keep on growing to their unfathomed ends.

On positive side these ever-growing chains of actions & reactions definitely have benefited us psycho-biologically. We have developed our body, mind and intellect enough to tackle this ever increasing load of actions. But difficulty is we are now helpless to have freedom of choice of action. Our freedom to choose actions is restricted. We are helpless to find free will. We are continuously being programmed by both accomplished and unaccomplished actions and we only follow reactions which are predetermined and they keep occupied our minds. Doing so we exhibit a tendency to behave like puppets in the hands of secret nature. It has just become hard for us to choose one action of our choice and happily perform it without any consequential remainder. The psycho-biological continuity of action binds us. Our psychic reactions to the outside happenings take root as conditioned reflexes. Spiritual disciplines do boast to cause de-programming of these action-reaction sequences. They even boast to completely end this *karmic chain.*

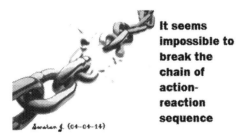

It seems impossible to break the chain of action-reaction sequence

Certain spiritual practices identify actions needed for acquiring that inner freedom but without telling you how to be free of them later! Practice itself may become your bondage. Perhaps that is why many spiritual traditions as a way to get freedom from bondage of actions call us not to perform action at all i.e. to take leave from the world and renounce it; lead a subliminal life hidden and uninvolved from rest of world and depend upon the subsistence from others, door to door collection of alms for survival. That means to become a *sanyasin,* a renunciate for the simple reason to break the chain of consequences. But where would go the actions which created renunciation as a consequence. Isn't that a part of some previous long chain too! Also being *sanyasin* definitely is not a panacea for whole of mankind so some other ways must be looked into.

What separates man from his biological counterparts, i.e. the animals, is not his ability to react but his ability to reflect. Both man and amoeba are at the extreme ends of evolutionary chain and both are forms of conscious life on earth. They are not inert because they are biologically and chemically alive. They respond to environmental changes not merely as chemicals but also as conscious life. Amoeba for example responds to change in pH of the water in which it swims and moves away from highly acidic or alkaline contents, so is man who would always take shelter from extremes of weather and other harshest conditions of nature.

This simple observation shows consciousness in action in us. Consciousness is always there for our survival. But while amoeba is simply conscious of the environment and reacts accordingly, man is not only conscious of environment but also conscious of himself at the same time. He can think over and analyze his acts. He can deduce and reason out the inferences. He can change the course of his life in the light of his previous reactions.

Simply this means man can reflect over happenings. This ability of man to reflect is quite primitive. All our tools of reading and writing developed over time are our aids to reflection. When a man for the first time narrated story of his encounter with some wild animal to his fellows he actually reflected over his immediate past. Man invented language and speech and letters for writing which are all one or other forms of reflection. He created timeless poetry and tales for the generations to come and put in his thoughts both past and future elements. Primitive man also reflected over happenings through drawings and cave paintings.

There could be different ways of reflection. Contemplation over the past foregone acts, analyzing their meaning, drawing conclusions, putting them in categories, using them as references, weighing future actions in the light of previous ones, are some of our prime reflections. We gather knowledge, solve problems, grow intellectually and become wise through reflection. Such reflections have certainly played their part for the development of the civic world but do these have some role for the development of our inner world. These reflections are over the actions of the past, performed already and contemplation upon them may not free us from the consequences of our action and may not even change them despite efforts. By reflecting over past we may increase level of intellect but not awareness. The logical remedy is to do something at the moment the action is performed.

The consequential effect of an action can be joyful if the action performed was good and charming one and it becomes depressing if the action performed was disgusting personally as well as socially. One generally asks himself what he personally gained from performing that action, praise or condemnation, sin or virtue, good or bad feeling, revengeful or do good type mentality. These fruits are psychological outcomes and are unnecessarily attached to the actions we perform and we happily feed on them. To ignore these effects on our psyche is difficult because we are already pre-programmed to categorize our actions as good or bad as per social value system. Above all we are always a part of an institution or a family, educational or social or political and we cannot afford to refuse the legal and social consequences of our actions. Howsoever mentally tough we might be but as a performer of an action we are strongly attached to the reactions our actions had invited from others. Even after performance of an action we eagerly look for the residual reactions in others. If our action harms someone we feel disgusted and we are happy if our actions were praised by the society. We can never refuse the feeling, this mental pleasure or sorrow that accompanies our actions. The psychic effect of joviality or melancholy in minor or major degrees is bound to follow our every action. Such effects bind us to the actions we perform.

So spirituality advises us to beware of this. Spirituality advises us to be a witness of actions at the time of performance. Witness depicts a neutral doer, may be another part of psyche, a hidden observer who supervises the worldly doer without interfering in his activities. In the end perhaps at the time of death you are advised to do away with your worldly doer and take back the witness as real you which will transmigrate to next life without consequence of your actions of this life. Without going to many details this may be the crux of the spiritual philosophy held by so many current and ancient spiritual traditions. This is true or not, nobody has reported after death. This may not be the remedy for this life but of some after life, science as well as we people have not got proof.

In another way people may completely stop performing actions and may become *sanyasin*. How much logical that would be? Is it true spirituality? Wouldn't that action of becoming neutral performer be a reaction to some other secret action developed inside your psyche? And even more than that after becoming *sanyasin* would you be able to stop yourself acting or reacting altogether? Won't you be still a part of the world but in some different place and situation and of course in some different institution other than family?

It appears clear that it is very difficult for us to stop our actions becoming our unending mental chain of reactions or consequences and ultimately becoming our bondage. Throughout the history of man, mankind has adopted different ways to get freedom from mental consequences of their actions but without any degree of success. They have erected churches, formed monasteries, raised religions, formulated laws, shun married and other forms of social life put themselves in rigorous discipline and isolation but were never capable of freeing themselves from bondages of human actions. Only death frees us from such bondage they have concluded.

Now examining this entire scenario in another way, seeing anything before us is an act of observance. We act as an observer to examine the objects we see, hear or feel. We observe different things of this universe and make them object of our study. Object of our observance may be a material substance, or a piece of philosophical thought. You can study your own body to see what it is made of and how you can modify it in case of illness. You can study mind and see how it behaves alone and in presence of others. You can study a thought and its etymological origin. There seems no end to such observance which we group under various sciences. You can study human behavior and develop ethics or laws to stop us going to the animal kingdom. But can our observations touch our own being? Can you objectify your own spirit; can you observe your own observer? Crux of the spirituality lies on this point.

You will never be able to objectify your own soul, howsoever hard you try. In science while you do the experiments you set up an observational field. Here you are an observer and you observe the results of the experiments you performed and make objective observations and conclude the results. Here observer as a scientist studies by remaining away from the observational field. The classical Newtonian physics maintains this duality, the separation of observer and the observed. Scientist as an observer is subject while the things he observes are the object. He studies the objects. Much of our science is the objective science. So does the Newton and his Physics.

All our subsidiary sciences including medical science are products of Newtonian physics which takes assumption of an external reality that can be observed and described. Scientific rules can be formulated and calculation can be done with many physical variables. It assumes an observer scientist and the observed field. They both lie at two separate points. Scientist while observing the observed object always remains away and do not merge within the object. One may observe a closer object as his heart or his palpitations or a thought in his brain or his headache, but these seem coming from some distant field or organ which we seem trying to objectify.

The fundamental assumption of Newtonian physics is that the objective world exists independently of any observations that are made on it. This setting makes observer and observed field as dual pair. This is the observer-observed duality. Observational field external to the senses is not the sole reality of the universe. When a scientist moves in a quantum realm or sees quantum reality as a unified whole he observes the limitations of his learned science i.e. Newtonian Physics[2]. For solving this dilemma of observer-observed duality new science proposed the Quantum theory of Physics[3].

---

[2]   **Sir Isaac Newton, (1642-1727)**, was mathematician and physicist, one of the leading scientific intellectual of our times. **Classical mechanics** and **Quantum Mechanics** are the two major sub-fields of Physics. Classical mechanics or Newtonian Physics is concerned with the set of laws describing the motion of bodies observed from a distance under the action of a system of forces. The study of the motion of bodies is an ancient one, making classical mechanics one of the oldest and largest subjects in science.

[3]   **Quantum mechanics** (QM—also known as **quantum physics**, or **quantum theory**) is a branch of physics which deals with physical phenomena at sub-atomic level where the action is on the order of the Planck Constant. It departs from Classical mechanics primarily at the **Quantum Realm** which

Quantum theory takes into consideration of reality as one single observational field or a quantum whole. The objects which we perceive are mere observational defects i.e. when observer objectifies his own field externally without mergence into field of reality. Quantum physics makes observer as part of reality or observed field. It does not divide reality into subjective and objective parts. It takes away the duality and makes non-dual reality as single uniformity of universe. In pure physical terms Newtonian observations behave better when applied to macroscopic (outer) aspect of things, it is said. But at the subatomic level these theories don't hold any success.

This new theory of the Quantum physics was proposed to take away observer observed duality and put you in a quantum realm as single reality of the universe. You can say that you observe this universe but you also know at the same time that you are the part of reality and not separate as an observer. Here observer is the part of the act of observance. Between the observer and observed there is no thinking mind, the worldly ego or a philosophical thought or mathematical calculation. Observer is simply aware of the reality and grasps it without thinking mind. There is no intermediation what so ever. This makes all the separate points of reality, the men, the animals and other physical objects as one single quantum whole.

What this all means in terms of spirituality. Here observer and the observed field are one. The consciousness is the

---

is the 'observer and observed' reality merging into quantum wholeness at sub-atomic level. Source: http://en.wikipedia.org/wiki/Classical_mechanics

observer field and the subject who holds consciousness is the observer. It is his individual consciousness getting a fine merger in his own field of awareness and then in the whole universe, then in the universal consciousness. At this stage he himself becomes not just part of but the whole of universal consciousness. This thought is akin to the ancient Indian philosophy of Upanishads or Vedanta.

Objectifying God is like objectifying your own soul by you as observer. You can make object your body, even your ego, your personality but not the consciousness. Consciousness cannot be made object because you act from the consciousness. You are the consciousness within the matter. It is the subject. So God is also not object. It is the subject. Observer and observed field are actually one. There is unswerving continuity from you to the universe, claims Quantum Theory of Physics.

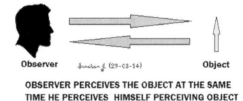

Observer *Sundaran J. (29-03-14)* **Object**

OBSERVER PERCEIVES THE OBJECT AT THE SAME TIME HE PERCEIVES HIMSELF PERCEIVING OBJECT

In traditional religious India there are two thoughts regarding this. One is that of *Dvaita*, the duality, which maintains that God is an objective entity separate from the creation and if you want to reach Him, you must raise temples, form statues and pray before him and do many similar other practices. Men and other jiva-s i.e. the life forms have come to the earth because of their past sins. The life is an act of punishment pronounced by divine etc.

Advent of new Upanishad

etc. Other thought is of *Advaita*, of non-duality, which says that no such duality exists between man and God and man's individual consciousness is but the universal consciousness manifested. Great proponent of this theory was Adishankaracharya[4], an 8th century Indian mystic and interpreter of spiritual treatises, Upanishads and Gita, who lived life of only 33 years. His idea of wholeness of reality is what the science has discovered today through quantum physics. There is one single reality of universe and man and other diverse creations are manifested phenomenal world, Maya or simply an untruth. So man is both a part of phenomenal world as Maya i.e. his physical body but as consciousness he is nothing but God, the universal soul.

The consciousness is pure interiority exterior of which is unknown, says Sartre[5] greatest philosopher of our times.

---

[4] **Adi Shankaracharya (788-820)** Adi Shankaracharya or the first Shankara, the teacher, was a remarkable re-interpreter of Hindu scriptures, Upanishads and Vedanta. He had a profound influence on the growth of Indian thought at a time when chaos, superstition and bigotry was raging.

The phenomenal world of beings and non-beings is not apart from the Brahman but ultimately become one with Brahman, he preached. The crux of Advaita is that Brahman alone is real, and the phenomenal world is unreal or an illusion. Through intense practice of the concept of Advaita, individual ego and thought of God and soul as two can be removed from the mind of man. Source: http://en.wikipedia. org/wiki/Adi_Shankara

[5] **Jean Paul Sartre (1905-1980):** His philosophical career focuses, in its first phase, upon the construction of a philosophy of existence known as existentialism. "What do we mean by saying that existence precedes essence? We mean that man first of all exists, encounters himself, surges

This simple statement infers that the entire objective world is within the ambit of consciousness.

By claiming so, science has incorporated the variable of consciousness in the study of matter. Fred Alan Wolf[6], a pioneer of Quantum physics writes, "The universe is not just a collection of separate points. It is what it is according to the observer and what he or she does. By identifying with the 'quantum wholeness' of the world, the observer becomes the observed. He is what he sees."

In very simple terms this means that if one day by any means when we are enlightened, we are able to understand this universe, the reality, God and observe everything before us, what would we see? We would be looking at ourselves; or say there would just awareness without objectivity. This act of observance is an act of very superior reflection. This reflection is different from our routine reflections of reading and writing where we objectify our knowledge. It is different from analyzing past activities. It is different from the conclusions and inferences drawn from collected knowledge.

---

up in the world—and defines himself afterwards. If man as the existentialist sees himself not definable, it is because to begin with he is nothing. He will not be anything until later, and then he will be what he makes of himself." He writes in "Existentialism is Humanism". Source: http://www.iep.utm.edu/sartre-ex/

[6] **Fred Alan Wolf (born 1934)** is an American theoretical physicist specializing in quantum physics and the relationship between physics and consciousness. He is author of many books including '*Taking the Quantum Leap*'.

There always remains an object away from the subject as outer observational field. To make this subject an object of study you need a different approach. It is entirely difficult to make subject the object. How would you create a oneness principle guiding the two. In the laboratory the spirituality or quantum wholeness subject is you and observer of the subject is also you. What you do here is not observance but a sort of meta-observance, not simple perception but an apperception. Apperception is the perception of the perception. You do the perception to perceive the outer world and you do apperception to perceive your own perceptions. This act of apperception is not subsidiary to perception or follows it; both run alongside and occur at the same time.

Emanuel Kant, German philosopher[7], in his 18th century classic 'Critique of Pure Reason' writes more on apperception and distinguishes *empirical apperception* from *transcendental*

---

[7]   **Immanuel Kant (1724-1804)** is one of the most influential philosophers in the history of Western philosophy. His contributions to metaphysics, epistemology, ethics, and aesthetics have had a profound impact on almost every philosophical movement that followed him. In one of his most important works, *The Critique of Pure Reason* Kant addresses the question "What can we know?" The simplified answer is that 'our knowledge is constrained physical aspects of the natural, empirical world. It is impossible, Kant argues, to extend knowledge to the supersensible realm of speculative metaphysics. The reason that knowledge has these constraints, Kant argues, is that the mind plays an active role in constituting the features of experience and limiting the mind's access only to the empirical realm of space and time. Source: http://www.iep.utm.edu/kantmeta/

apperception. The first one is "the consciousness of the concrete actual self with its changing states". You may call it "inner sense". You regularly apperceive your inner states i.e. state of happiness or sorrow. You are affected by these and you change your external perception in light of these.

The second is "the pure, original, unchangeable consciousness which is the necessary condition of experience as such and the ultimate foundation of the synthetic unity of experience". This means that consciousness reflects over itself at the moment the action is performed or very precisely at all times as there in no moment when consciousness is not performing any action. It is a continuous act of knowing a contemporary to perception, before you collect it as knowledge and memory and as thoughts. You perceive your inner states in their purity and are not affected by them.

The idea of apperception is to capture the moment in its current situation, neither its immediate past nor the immediate future. Best way to understand apperception is to observe consciousness at work. While you perform an action what you do? You either perform an action or you will watch how the action is being performed. It is very difficult to perform both actions at the same time. You cannot deliberately watch yourself performing action.

You make mistakes when someone is watching you performing an action. Half of your attention is involved in watching other, how one is being looked at, will be praised or not etc. etc. This is an act of becoming self conscious and not the action of reflection or being conscious of the act. But if your actions are not being watched from another angle these will become unconscious. Most of your actions are unconscious in a way that you come to know about them when the action has been performed. Actions performed in self absorbed person, alone in dream like state are unconscious actions.

While typing a document you make many spelling mistakes which you later on correct. This is because you put your awareness to wandering thoughts and not to the typing. The level of awareness where you are open not only to the act but also to the information coming from thought activity makes you aware, super-aware or unaware person. To learn primarily how one can perform activities and at the same time be aware of it spirituality advises us to keep the number of actions performed at a time minimum as possible. That is the idea to make one's life simple. To apperceive the consciousness, they advise us to be neutral and still for some time and watch the inner self.

While doing this you are not performing any outer activity so you look for the activity in your head, in your brain. Activity of the thoughts is also the activity of your consciousness. You observe your thoughts. They arise as ripples in the still lake of the consciousness. If you are affected by the mental state of joy or sorrow the thoughts create then you are apperceiving empirically as Kant describes. But if you experience the thought activity the moment it arise in the stillness of the brain without becoming aware to the affect the thought create or state of joy or sorrow you feel but you become aware of your state of awareness only then you are doing transcendental apperception. That is what spiritualists say of meditation. Thoughts are merely outer surface activity of this act of meditation and if you consistently watch your thoughts they will subside after some time.

You are then one to one with your consciousness. You merge in your consciousness. Here one could watch all his reactions before putting them to action or even before they manifest. One can modify or de-program the stereotyped thoughts and reactions. In actuality you do not do this yourself as an active doer but they are automatically de-programmed. That is a state of peaceful bliss. At this state there is merger of experience-er with the experience, see-er with the scene, observer with the observed. The vast expanse of consciousness is before you and you now transcend from your meager earthly existence to your universal existence.

— 0 —

(2)

Some Initial Preparations
(Bid farewell to conceptual frame of mind first!)

We ideate and conceptualize; we learn and grow intellectually. We conceptualize to make things better understandable. Ideas and concepts are two much loved things our mind feeds on. New thoughts enter the mind as ideas. Ideas are conceived as flashes of insight. They take origin as insight. These are the long lost knowledge of mankind which is reminded to us occasionally. These are the internal visualization of the mind. And why not, 'idea' means to see internally (in Greek).

Idea is a very fragile little thing. It has a very little life of its own. It occurs as a flash in the mind, remains ambiguous and cryptic unless intellectualized and given a worldly language. It won't stay forever with you unless you solidify it with the 'clay' of concept. And what are these concepts? These are the frameworks of the things known already. Since childhood we have been taught to create and nurture concepts in the mind. We intellectualize by putting our ideas into the known conceptual frames. We weigh any new idea by our previously scripted concepts.

Should we say for now that we already have a 'preferred position' for understanding new? Our concepts have given us the basic argumentative position as our premise. We call them as our standing principals and we have collected them since very beginning of all learning or as a basis of all reasoning we were bestowed with. All our reactions and reasons, our inferences and conclusions are build on that basis! So bad luck indeed, new (idea) has mixed with the old (concepts) and lost its novelty. We have not grown an inch more, maybe we have found a new explanation, a new theory, or a new argument.

Our concepts create all our pre-judgments and prejudices even. They cause our intellect to grow in our own sweet way. As we become more intellectual, more and more concepts creeps in, more and more we become a subject position and more and more we lose position as a conscious subject. That's right we can argue well but to openheartedly embrace an alternative idea or different opinion is difficult. We used to be one who was open to new ideas and new information in our younger days. We were intelligent then but not intellectual. As we grow intellectual old and dead information thwarts the entry of the new. Our intellect started filtering the information and restricts a part which enters without known frames.

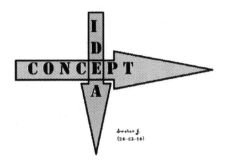

Figure: Not running parallel! Ideas cross vertically the previously learned concepts

We then become product of our own text written by our own hands. We do not speak but we are spoken; spoken by the quantity of information we collect in our head. Our life becomes a scripted event. We are the authors of this script and we ourselves put it into action in life. We always have a voice in the head, voice of authors we have read, voice of thoughts that we've collected, voice of beliefs we've harbored. This voice we hold both individually and collectively as a race. We speak from this voice. How then is to speak from the silence, from our own inner centrality we might have never wondered? Where has gone novelty in your life, sometimes we ask surprisingly. But none other than us have shut the doors of life's unique insights.

Perhaps that is why new idea never renews us. We never feel the vibration while we encounter a new insight. We never feel the need to go beyond your old shriveled concepts. We have devised readymade answers to our readymade problems. Our problems are textual and answers are conceptual. Problems we talk most often are not found in the struggling world!

We are well off worldly, sound mentally, reasonable philosophically but still we are not original. We are trapped in our understanding and prisoner of thoughts. We are swayed by our own persuasions before we try to persuade others.

Concepts construct our intellectual boundary. This is the point from where our intellectual blindness starts. This happens when we encounter new things. We simply term new information fantastic, we may even argue over some obvious aspects of it. But we will have to admit that we cannot understand, not even comprehend. It is difficult for us to visualize new ideas with our old spectacles. We simply have cultured the habit of rearranging known intellectual themes to produce new thoughts.

Concepts take roots as our unconscious beliefs. They settle down at deeper layers of the mind. They become an unconscious force compelling us to make an opinion before every happening. We pre-judge every situation or at least try to. We usually say 'I know that; I have the idea; all things happen that way'. We not only suppose but validate every guess of ours before happening. We are happy when things happen according to our supposition. We blame nature when unexpected things come up. To escape from this we try to live a life of certainty. We fear the field of uncertainty.

So this is the reality that we avoid. When we have already avoided 'the truth' in our outer life how would we ever face truth of our inner life? Your unconscious and subconscious mind has many uncertain truths. But we never face them. We never visit them. We have tendency to live life superficially in order not to experience inner void. This simply turns into dark area of our psyche.

These dark areas of our inner world become darker day by day. We visit them occasionally in our dreams. That reality is fearful. For smooth sailing we create a busy life. This is life of borrowed and invented truths. All the opinion we gather about God, spirit, sin and virtues are our invented truths, they are not real. We have invented the ideas of inner world and we believe in them. Our protracted following of these ideas has invented for us certain doctrines and associated rituals and we pass the entire life carrying them in our heads.

Do we ever free ourselves from invented concepts altogether? Do we ever de-conceptualize our thoughts?

Non-conceptual understanding is a sort of immediate understanding. Here we don't understand but feel the thoughts, feel the ideas as they move within. We feel the thoughts first and just wait to understand them or make a conclusion. We don't counter the thought with another thought with argumentation or explanation. We culture a different habit of understanding thoughts without even words.

This is to put our awareness to learn first before our knowledge catches reality like an eagle catches its prey. We feel it and not speak about it. A single word uttered within mind when you look at some marvelous will contaminate its excellence. This marvelous may be anything—a great thought, a great deed or wonderful words of wisdom.

The reality we know or understand is not the reality out there. Our reality is the reality of our thoughts. We have kept it contained by our thoughts by the definitions and concepts. We need not define the reality to understand it. We simply need to experience it. This is the intuitive perception that goes into the 'hearty brain' bypassing the 'intellectual heart'. This is the awakening of non-mind, the mind within mind that understands without words. There is a good difference between one's own understanding of reality and the real reality. Non-conceptual understanding simply clarifies this.

You must resist knowing. Not knowing is also a virtue. Life is a mystery. It is charming to those who do not know their next moment. You must equally resist intellectualizing, or understanding theoretically. You may feel the things inside. To heighten the feeling level is the indispensable quality for generating intuitive wisdom.

Intuitive perception is the inner vision. Intuition is prophetic vision and is available to us only once we learn to work with transparent consciousness. The persons with cunning motives may not find it.

Intuition is the perception of same consciousness working in us which collects information as knowledge. It collects and processes the information. It is the refined processing rather. The bits of information knowledgeably processed enter into the knowledge chain. The rest unsaved information still under process may be received as intuition if we allow our mind to relate that way. Whole of the city may be in danger. Only the prophet conveys the right thing to do by the ruler or citizens at the turbulent times.

Prophets of yore have left their time. They have given you the basic understanding to comprehend reality. But you cannot put all their solutions to your current situations. Now you are the prophet of your life. Now you need to culture the prophetic vision.

Fire is hot is repeated thousand times by your teachers, guides and masters and it only results in concretizing our concepts. Only when we come across the fire and realize it ourselves we break our concepts and move a small step toward de-conceptualization.

What this idea of de-conceptualization holds to our understanding of spirituality. All this does not mean you altogether bid farewell to intellectual brain. We simply need to realize the information processing by the brain on daily basis. How the brain compartmentalizes the information by making folders and subfolders. The information we need for worldly matters would go to intellectual compartment.

But the almost all the information for intuitive mind must be processed at the feeling level. We must not blunt these feelings. We must never slow down our awareness. Life's gravest mistakes occur during laziness. There is great deal of descriptions of spirituality in our scriptures. All religious philosophies are purely conceptual. They describe rather than present before us cognitive aspects of reality. But there is intuitive side of us which we have missed due to intellectual predominance in our affairs. Consciousness cannot be described—it must be known directly without mediation of concepts. If our mind feeds more on cooked & conceptual thoughts then spirituality becomes a matter of understanding and its similar proliferation in our mind. But the same thought can be used to awaken ourselves to altogether unknown realities.

— 0 —

(3)

Knowing the Unknowable-
(Perceiving Eye within the Eye)

If someone says "I have seen God" should we ask him how he has done so? Whether he has seen God physically or deduced philosophically; has he begot God at the feeling level or found in the books, in the temples or in his thoughts; has he seen God with external eyes or seen with his inner vision? So far people have indulged in similar ventures.

God is unknowable for us all. This is all too strange that while every one of us is deeply interested in search of the unknowable still very few keep up their interest up to a certain degree. People want to know the reality of God even while they keep themselves indulged in worldly affairs. Those who search not only want to search God for them but also desire to tell others about their search. They want to write books, articles and journals, web pages about their expedition and usually spend a lifetime to prove their hypothetical ideas.

To speak of the God in fact is not to speak of God of reality if there ever has been any such God. When you speak about

God you are talking about God of your thoughts. God which is in your thoughts can't be the real God. What is in your thoughts is the concept of God. God of thoughts that may be in any person howsoever wise he may be can't be the real God. The real God is something called truth or reality of universe a part of which is directly before you and a part perhaps a major part you can't figure out with ordinary observations. To comprehend the truth or reality as a whole you'll have to go to some other realm away from ordinary thought process.

A thought is a physiological process just like any other process in your body viz. digestive or respiratory. It is part of chemical activity or more so neuro-transmitter change in the neuronal synapses. So thought is a matter. Thought as matter is a part of manifest reality as your body and brain. This realty seen outside is available to the senses and our physical instruments. The same exists as physical processes that we find in our body or brain or mind.

Beyond our mind and in inner depths of consciousness there is the non-manifest reality. This reality is not touched by thoughts or physical gadgets. Thought may imagine or reify the reality. But we as consciousness are connected to the deeper levels of reality. This realm still not matter in the correct physical sense and is endlessly interconnected with universal reality including all physical and live matter. This reality is not definable.

This reality is not understandable. When you define it becomes mere understanding through concepts of your mind. When you say anything about it you start imagining it first and later on understanding and believing your own imagination. We must understand that a thought is a part of reality not complete reality. We along with our thoughts along with this entire neutral universe make this reality a one complete whole. We cannot observe reality by shifting away from whole. When we see something before our eyes we overlook our back; we overlook the floor and roof; we overlook the looking interior. Anything fragmented from the whole can't be the complete reality. The problem with observance via thought is that it observes by moving away from whole and creating observer-observed duality. So the thought merely brags to speak of the reality, a part of which is mere confabulation and imagination.

Thus a thought can imagine or form an idea of the non-manifest reality. But actual relation of thought and deeper mind is the relation of mind to the inner energy of emptiness from which thought emerges. Once this thought leaves the steering position and takes a back seat or subside, we actually can have the contact with the non-manifest at the cognitive level. But once the thought is in arena of perception of reality it immediately changes or strives to change it as per its own idea or view. It may suddenly become fearful and would strive to view reality in different colors.

But this is certain we cannot change the reality, we can only change the view of reality. We can merely mask reality with our thoughts. We cannot at all think of the ways to change or modify the internal reality. If at all we seem to modify it is the reality of our mind. Mind or thought simply changes the way for us to perceive in cordial manner. For tough and harsh external reality we tend to substitute it with more amiable one.

We arrive at the real reality not through thoughts or forming theories but going beyond thoughts. For this internal reality to comprehend we simply have to witness. And we witness all e.g. one that is available as reality to our senses and other available to our feelings or cognition of it and still other available to our thoughts, to our understanding.

Unknowable is not the thing beyond. This is one typical effort of the knower to know the knower. When the knower makes an effort to know himself, the knower will have to go to the feeling level. Now if he wants to narrate his findings he will have to take mediation of thoughts in some comprehensible language. Otherwise his feelings will not be comprehended.

Unknowable is the dilemma of a baby fish, who asked her mother fish one day after enjoying a nice swim,

"Where is that sea I hear from others?"

"Fool, this is just what is around you!"

"Oh! But I can't see it."

"You don't have to see it; you'll have to experience it."

Unknowable is not some hidden entity or something immersed in our own subatomic fields and we've to dig it with instruments. This is also not an abstract philosophical or scientific theme or hidden knowledge and we have to go to knowledge archives to excavate it. Our eyes can see every other thing in the world, but not themselves. Eye cannot see the eye. Seer cannot see himself. Seer of the objects is trained to look at objects but not at him.

If ever this seer takes a position to see his own being. Can he do so comfortably? This seer which sees is unknowable for the seer. The actual position of seer is the blind spot for the seer. This becomes a hidden entity for him. When we close our eyes what we see is void within. We not only see the void we also experience the void.

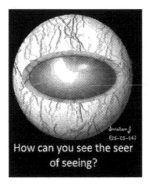

How can you see the seer of seeing?

"Likewise the void is what you right now don't see when you try to look at Brahm'. The void is exactly what you have always looked for and have always never found or seen," writes Ken Wilber[8], this century's most prominent spiritual philosopher with scientific leaning.

Similarly Upanishads which are ancients India's wonderful treatise for self knowledge say in a brilliant most expression-

How can you see the seer of the seeing?

---

[8] **Kenneth Earl "Ken" Wilber II** (b.1949) is an American writer and public speaker. He has written and lectured about mysticism, philosophy, ecology and development psychology. His work formulates what he calls Integral Theory. In 1998 he founded the Integral Institute.

Knowing the Unknowable-

(Brihadaryanaka Upnishad-III: 2)[9]

Unknowable is similarly unknowable to the knower when the knower attempts to know itself. This is as same as soul is unknowable for the soul and God would be unknowable for the God. If God ever desire to know his own nature course it would be difficult for Him to know what He is. Thus man who is nothing but the supreme manifestation of the God perceives God as unknowable. This unknowable is man himself! Every conscious subject has a hidden entity. This entity is where he himself exists.

For making knowable the unknowable we will have to move to another position. We may start using a simple tool which is available to all of us i.e. our mind. Our mind is a wonderful instrument. Akin to modern days computers it is both input and output device. It is the window, just like window operating system of our computer. It is connected with both the devices of computer i.e. on one side with

---

[9] **The Upanishads** are a collection of Vedic texts which contain the earliest emergence of some of the central philosophical concepts Indian thought collectively compiled as Vedanta (the end of the Veda). *Brhadaranyaka Upanishad* means the "great forest-book"—meaning that is should be read in solitude. In Chapter 3, Brahmanas 1-4 sage Yājñavalkya says, "I cannot say, 'here is the Ātman; here is the Self'. It is not possible because—*na dṛṣṭer draṣṭāram paśyeḥ*—you cannot see the seer of seeing. The seer can see that which is other than the Seer, or the act of seeing. An object outside the seer can be beheld by the seer. How can the seer see himself? How is it possible?
Source: http://www.swami-krishnananda.org/brdup/brhad_III-01.html

output devices (keyboard and mouse) and on the other with the inner software. Computer cannot run without the monitor guide which is the inter-play of both. Similarly the mind is the monitor guide. It is the connecting link to inner consciousness and the outer world. Without mind we may never know there is consciousness. Or without the mind again, consciousness may never be able to relate with the world.

Our mind works in collaboration with the senses. These are input devices. Mind can take or discard any information according to the choice and fixation. Chosen information goes to memory stores. Mind is an instrument of experience. All our experiences in the world occupy the memory stores. These experiences when time and again put to practice in the world ultimately become our knowledge. One way of knowledge coming to the mind is from the perception by the senses. Mind stores for us the palpable knowledge of the things which we see, hear, taste, smell or feel about, a clear and direct perceptible knowledge.

There is another knowledge which is not direct but indirect. This knowledge is by inference. It is the knowledge of judgment and reason. The previous knowledge of things that we have, guides our future inferences regarding the same object. We can judge, analyze and draw the meaning of the things. This judgment, analysis or conclusions are the indirect knowledge of the world. The indirect knowledge of the things comes from our judgment, when we put the things under our own scrutiny. We analyze the things to find their real nature which means first to break them up. This means the themes are broken into parts and later on combined to form a meaningful logic.

Analysis is an approach applied extensively in philosophy and science. By this we reduce one substantial whole to smaller parts. By synthesis you join these well analyzed smaller components into a cohesive whole. Analysis and synthesis should be complementary to each other. Every analysis should be followed by synthesis and every synthesis should precede analysis. This is like peeling of the onion skin. You do it layer after layer and reached innermost or very inner layers. This is all analytical activity. Now in the end, if you do not reconstruct the onion what was the need to open it at the first place? From the root of knowledge from where we have started we have reached the most peripheral branch. Now we do not know our way to roots. We do not know this root. What a disgraceful expedition of knowledge! Synthesis is reaching this root again, reconstructing the onion again.

During early years we are much dependent upon the direct knowledge of the things. For ship we visit an actual ship or look at its photograph. With time as we age as weakness and lethargy strikes body, mind too becomes lethargic. It doesn't feel any need to have direct knowledge. Once all imagery of worldly objects, intellectual themes, and psychological principles are sufficiently engraved in the mind as a concept we do not feel an need to verify them. As we age we become dependent upon our indirect conceptual knowledge i.e. knowledge of judgments and inferences. Young people often wonder about knowledge of their elders. They wonder how easily they can reason out what they have done physically. This is just same as you observe in detective stories and see how detective agents solve the cases by mere observations and inferences.

Mature people draw abstractions and know the things philosophically. They create, nurture and later on become dependents upon their concepts. Their knowledge becomes theoretical. This is not fool proof as compared to direct knowledge because external objects and our understanding of them keep on changing. They may err in correctly creating and deciphering their theoretical knowledge. Much part of it remains old and stale if not updated with the current one. Only young people gather direct proof of the things. World is ever changing, so the old and mature people loose novelty of the things by relying upon their judgments only.

All analysis and synthesis activity is done to understand nature. It is done to dissect the nature. But this dissection is done by the thought activity. We dissect nature with our philosophical thoughts and scientific theories. But we must understand one thing. By thoughts or by thinking only we cannot see or experience reality. Thought cannot capture the reality of soul or God. Thought can capture only the understanding of reality.

There is another type of knowledge which is neither direct nor of the inferences. This is the direct experience of subtle things[10]. We can see the rose. But can we see the love when

---

[10]   **Aparokshanubhuti:**. Advent of knowledge in mind is via **pratyaksh**—i.e. direct experience, **proksh**—i.e. indirect or inferential knowledge and **Aproksh**. Aproksh can be literally described as **Direct Experience** of subtle things. It is a famous work attributed to Adi Shankracharya. It is a popular introductory work that expounds Advaita Vedanta philosophy. It describes a method that seekers can follow to directly experience the essential truth of one's one nature.

rose is—presented to someone. There may be hundred people in a gathering when a lover presents rose to his beloved. They all applaud. They can see the love. Some can feel love and some merely understand. Those who feel love might be more close to the person(s) concerned.

Love is there not as physically quantifiable property or a part of philosophical thought or even imagined one. The love cannot be materialized or conceptualized for our identification. This idea of love is not dependent upon collection of conceptual or analytical knowledge about love.

Perception of love occurs at feeling level. This can only be meta-cognized. This meta-cognition is more of a perception. It is like becoming neutral witness. This knowledge of knowledge is called realization. You will have to realize the things which are too subtle to be perceived as a physical object. To experience being at top of Mount Everest you'll have to directly experience and not to rely on accounts of others. Experience of things which are not in the external world happens in the subtle world. This is same directly realized knowledge. You may call it direct perception.

The soul or God, or love or hate, are realized at the level of heart, at level of feelings, at the level of soul. You cannot realize the love of another person towards some other unless you are not experiencing love at the same time. When you see your child loving and cuddling the dog, you cannot see love of one towards the other. You can only feel your love towards both. By feeling love at the same time three entities become one.

Same way you feel the hate or other similar feelings. If you don't feel it you merely understand it. Yes, you can realize your own love or hate. Soul which makes you, inside you, is similarly realized. But this one realization occurs at moment to moment basis. You cannot do it once and for all. One visualizes or meta-cognizes soul consistently as one moves in external reality. Once you realize your soul you feel it as you have realized God. You cannot realize God unless you have realized your own soul.

These types of things are never perceived by thinking. A Thought cannot capture the reality; it can capture the concepts of realty. Concepts are our manmade tools. They change with changing ages. They have changed since ancient to this present age. They won't remain same in the coming ages. But reality is not manmade. It was there forever and is now before our eyes. It is but outer and inner nature of universe. We can only describe or understand it through thoughts. The conceptual understanding is not realization. It is the indirect knowledge; knowledge of second kind.

For correct comprehension of reality we need the knowledge of third kind. The direct realization of reality is inward visualization. We see this creation taking origin, flourishing and dying and further recreating again. What we grasp the inner meaning of it. We need not conceptualize or analyze to get this meaning. It is happening before our eyes. We grasp the meaning with an urgency and immediacy, before your intellect enters the scene and gives you the conceptual knowledge of it.

What we visualize from above example is the imperishable nature of things. What we see is the universe of change. Buddha when got enlightenment called the whole world a compound phenomenon and declared compound phenomenon is always impermanent. Only elementary universe remain the same. This is knowledge of third kind. This does not need thinking mind. It is away from superficial or even deeper understanding. This deeper realization minus understanding is direct experience of reality.

Unknowable is something to be realized. It is not to be understood.

— 0 —

(4)

Silence—the Active Void Inside
(How then you Converse with your Silence)

There exists a still realm within deeper layers of consciousness far away from the worldly noise which you observe as inner silence. Silence is our deep inner core; transcending not only the mind or the body or consciousness but all three. Beyond our knowledge and intellect this still realm exists as timeless witness to human existence.

Still realm exists beyond the body and its chemicals; beyond atoms and subatomic space. Beyond mind and its thought activity; beyond the neurons; beyond all the electrochemical activity of the body, the silence exists. The matter as we understand is gross matter, it becomes finer and becomes the non-particle a pure form of energy which pervades the gross. It escapes the already occupied senses and mind is connected to it only when sensory apparatus is free and unoccupied. It is already there behind the veil of existence. It is not imaginary for it exists. It contributes to our activities (definitely!) and some of us may observe it at surface conscious level.

This still realm exists as silent contributor to our conscious activities. When you look at the lake, you notice the ripples on surface. But as you go down to its basin there are no ripples. They almost cease, come to naught. This silence of this still realm is similarly not solid or concrete. It is a lake inside and it is fluid and yet tranquil. It does not carry ripples, does not carry noise. Noise of thought activity and the ripples of knowledge are at the surface of it, where it becomes the stream (of knowledge) and flows in the world.

This inactive basin not simply there to provide a firm base for the active exterior but it does provide the necessary inputs to the fine activity running in the exterior. Though the activity in the firm base may not be perceptible but it is always active and energetic, always live. This is the magic box of magician. Only when you have a hearty talk with a very sincere friend you wonder from where you have got such a fine vocabulary, such a fine thoughts, such free and kind feelings.

Narrators of this silence are affectionate lovers of wisdom. They create and tell anecdotes of this inner silence. They love this quiet and active Sophia. They are the philosophers. They do not adore this wisdom goddess of from the outer. They don't objectify her. They worship her by going inside her, going even beyond their observable silence and becoming a real witness to the silent inner Sophia.

While you observe the still realm and while you communicate its activity to the outer you do need mediacy of thought. But you do not entertain the thought activity in already occupied mind. You have surface conscious thoughts guided by will and ego. You do not entertain the conscious knowledgeable thoughts. You make them silent first! You simply let them go and effortlessly communicate your inner silence! You become sheer conduit, a vehicle through which the silence passes on to outer. You rarely judge it with the existing value system. You rarely weigh it with your outer knowledge. You simply give words, the effortless, communicable and understandable words.

Your silence is a complete void inside you, the nothingness

These effortless words have their own concepts. They have their own reasonable logic. You don't further intellectualize or interpret them. When you do this and the silence time and again travels in your intellectual paths, the real contamination of silence occurs. The silence loses its pristine glory.

So you speak it but don't speak about it lest it become tainted with the mistaken and inadequate vocabulary. When you go there, you entertain nothing, not your mind even, your soul even. You don't express what you are witnessing; you don't speak what you have witnessed. You become just a dispassionate witness and just be there. Just as a lover who look at his beloved and not touch her.

Though this inner silence is still and tranquil activity and exists beyond thoughts and all turmoil and confusion of mind. Yet this inner stillness communicates. It comes to the surface. This becomes contemporary of your thoughts, not comes before or afterwards. You speak coherently your inner silence. If you are not coherent you are not speaking from your silence. You are speaking the words given by your will and ego, your knowledge and understanding. While communicating this type of thought activity you fumble most of the times.

At any time you can leave thoughts and move into stillness. Once in thoughtful mode this inner stillness does not thwart the thought activity.

Silence and thought go contemporary i.e. they occur at same time. Silence has dynamic stillness, neither complete motion nor complete immobility. It is equally active when thought is active. Silence creates thoughts but remain beyond thoughts. Thought is in active contact with the outer. Thought is also in active contact with silence. Thought is the intermediate.

Inner stillness gives necessary inputs to thoughts and makes them pointed or insightful. The surface thought activity interferes with its flawless expression. You will have to make silent this superficial brainy thought activity before you contact the inner silence. What happens when you are going to deliver an important lecture? You are loaded with the thoughts. For sometime in the beginning this surface thought activity interferes so much. But when silence is contacted in right way it will form its own thoughts. A person conveying those thoughts goes in trance himself. And also let other persons listening go in trance. All this happens in silence, yet activity is there. This is activity of silence in action.

Silence is delivering silence. This is an active silence.

When you are in meditation your thought activity cease, comes to naught. Silence becomes stillness non-active, without any thought. You are then with your silence; you have peace and bliss. You have a complete tranquility. You are in a happy stillness of mind, as says Wordsworth.

A person speaking from silence does not get tired of speaking. He does not deliberately construct his speech. He does not refer to his learned knowledge. He observes the outer and delivers his thoughts. He now speaks as the God's mind.

But arrhythmic thoughts loose contact with the silence. They go haywire. There occur so many branches of original thought that person does not know what he was speaking just a moment ago. He is baffled in his delivery of thoughts so does his audience.

Your silence is a complete void inside you, the nothingness. Your soul is the container of that void. The void is the container of your mind. Your mind is container of your thoughts. Your thoughts are container of your knowledge. Rest is all matter, the superficial worldly coverings of your real nature.

The void of the soul is continuous with the void of the universe. When you connect with this emptiness you actually connect with the universe. Here border line vanishes which was distinctly visible in the outer material body. You are one with the universe in an unbroken continuity. At the depth of the meditative state you observe all void. If you still visualize some images, of gods and deities, of gurus and guides, you are just not empty, just not silent. You are imagining like in a dream or in a hypnotized state. You have still not crossed the veil of mind and thoughts to enter this void.

This is an activity that resides in you. At any stage some thought may spurt from this silent depth. When a person form very superior thought or encounter a very superior insight, it comes from that silence. This one comes in the mind as spontaneous thought and it is observed when you are not involved with superficial thoughts. You speak directly from your consciousness. You become methodological when you speak from your knowledge. Here you turn worldly.

While in worldly mode you curb your own free thought activity. You kill your own freedom of speech. You speak as per requirement of time and audience. When mind observes objectively thoughts arise. The doubtful thought in response to the outer activity you later on collect as knowledge of the objects you see. This thought activity could present itself as spontaneous or as methodological manner.

Spontaneous thoughts arise from the silence. It is pure inner response to the outer, uncontaminated. This is the activity of pure awareness that resides in us. Spontaneous thoughts are always honest and straightforward.

Methodological thought comes into action when you start weighing outer situation with previous knowledge. It is artful, in order, with dry logic and may be crooked. The methodological thought arises from the activity of thinking mind, from the cultivated intellect. The methodological thought arises from cultured and shared wisdom, from knowledge we collected, from authors we read, from confusion we've created.

Silence is not muteness. Some of you observe disciplinary silence to curtail your thought activity. You observe silence for one or few days. This is unnecessary. Thoughts can never be kept silent for much time. You react and observe and make thoughts. The thought activity runs uninterrupted even during forced silence. When you do not speak to the outer you speak inside. You speak within your mind. You chat with your own brain.

Thoughts arising from silence are much less a learned activity. It is the inner guidance to us all. It is honest voice of ours. Knowledge merely gives a reasonable flow to this voice. However knowledge may twist its flow and make it practical for dealing with the world. Or it may entirely misguide us. It may entirely suppress the silent voice.

Perhaps that is why the inner silence speaks more clearly to those who are honest to themselves as well as to others. They may be illiterate, simple fellows or may have little worldly knowledge. But they have transparent soul. They are without excessive burden of their worldly ego and thinking mind.

How soundly we hear our inner voice? How often we contact our soul? This inner voice from silence may be jumbled and symbolic. But with transparency of soul we may be able to translate this reasonable voice of ours into worldly languages.

This inner silent voice may be voice of Moses or of Christ or some other prophet who are said to have talked with God. This may become your own inner voice.

— 0 —

(5)

Nature of Soul

(The Essence of Matter)

Nature of something can be said as its essence. Essence of the matter is age old philosophical question.

There is something called substance and there is something called essence. Essence is the nature of substance. An acidic compound is a substance, being acidic is its essence. An honest man is a substance and honesty is his essence. A savage population is a substance and savagery is its essence.

Physical body is a substance and soul is its essence.

Is it the same essence which emanates from the most of material substances as fragrance or as smell? Is it the real nature of substance or it is something else? Or does this word essence mean an abstract representation?

As you see in a full bloomed flower. You call its fragrance the essence. But again this is physical part of the body of flower, left by the flower to reach distant insects; to let them smell its presence. This scent is part of the flower.

But a flower is not altogether its essence, its fragrance. Flower is even more than that. Flower is a life form, a living substance, having innate intelligence. It directs its chemicals not only to convey its presence to others but also to convey its reproductive maturity. By emanating its essence it does not want to remain hidden even when it is not visible e.g. in the dark. By emanating essence it also creates around it a physical and emotional or better say sensational field. Does this flower and its essence one and same and do they exist contemporarily, at the same time?

Isn't it the flower which blooms to spread its essence in the environment existed earlier than its essence? Isn't the seed which existed even earlier with a motive to procreate new plant? Seed has created plant followed by the flower and then essence? Didn't the consciousness or say life in the seed which transmigrated genetically from earlier plant exist in the seed? It existed even earlier in the previous plants?

Does the existence follows or precedes the essence? Who came first the matter i.e. existence or consciousness. Which is the essence of whom?

Or better say who has planted the plant?

Is the soul progenitor of matter or its produce? Is not the honesty or savagery came into existence after a set of human population stayed put and existed together in a competitive mode? Or was this honesty or savagery primarily the choice of consciousness to exist in that way?

Life compulsorily arises in the matter when its atoms and molecules organize biologically in a particular way! So can we say—plant itself has planted the plant! None other than matter has created consciousness! None other than consciousness has organized matter!

Age old philosophical questions—does the substance which is a matter hides or reveals its essence?

Does our soul remain hidden behind the veil of physical body? Does this body which is matter is a mere covering which hides its real nature, its soul, its essence? Something beyond the comprehension of day to day activity of our senses! Is it extrasensory? Does it lie beyond the ordinary perception or thinking? Is it hidden from most sophisticated physical instruments even? Does it need an extraordinary ability of mind or senses to decipher or understand it or visualize it. But this may be entirely wrong for us to give such hidden attributes to the soul.

Does the essence of flower remain hidden? Does the honesty or savagery of men remain hidden?

Matter does not hide but reveals its essence. The soul is also not hidden behind layers of the body.

You can perceive the body by direct seeing, touching or tasting. A blind person feels the presence of another nearby without actually touching. Both blind and hearing impaired person also feels the presence of others.

You know there it is around you an environment, the space, the bodies! This is me and there are so many other bodies around me.

Even while you are lying with eyes closed you know your limbs. You know your heart. You know your brain. When they ache you know them. You know your body's normal and abnormal functions.

But what about its essence! What about its soul! What is the real nature of the soul? Can you see or feel it in the same manner as you see the outer body?

Is soul another function of the body? Is soul the presence of you while you don't exactly visualize your physical body? Same can be said of other bodies.

The real essence of existence is the presence in totality. The existence as a whole! This all does not imply only abstract existence, understandable rationally by intellectual themes. It is not mere meaning of existence, all hows and whys of the presence. It is existence by creating sensation and feeling. We exist beyond the comprehension or knowledge of human intellect. We exist in nature. We exist and convey our existence to co-existent. We spread our essence.

If essence of the body is soul, does this essence emanate from the gross body or does the gross body is guard of the inner essence?

The real essence of us is the wholeness of our existence. Some call it the spirit. People have called it so in the past. Soul is described in terms of spirit. Spirit conveys its meaning as absence of something which used to exist as a gross body. We say so of great men who left the world physically. Spirit or alcohol is something which used to exist as a copious matter before distillation process made it fine and small. Does the spirit of existent men have same meanings as the spirit or alcohol?

Spirit of dead person is called the subtle body. But how much of it is subtle? Is it quantifiable? Exists as matter or non-matter when it was the part of physical body! Anything that exists in nature is matter; anything that exists in our thoughts is non-matter. Non-matter is just imagination. If soul or spirit is not thought it must have existence in the body however subtle or sub-atomic it may be. It must be matter in strict scientific sense.

Otherwise it is merely the mental image of the body or bodies known to us. People perceive these images in their mind and keep on perceiving even after they leave physically. Why people only perceive those who are known to them. When they are near they perceive them as objects and when they are not near they feel their presence in their thoughts, in their imagination. They may even visualize them as image. Word imagination has the same root as the image. But this mental images or imaginations are phenomenon of the mind. We may be experiencing this because of hypnotized mind which is nothing but unconscious passionate attachment to the outer. We may be wrongly attributing these images to some super-natural powers. We cannot give such attributes to soul.

Nature of the body is revealed through its function, automation. Through its thoughts and ideas, behavior, actions, sensations, feelings the body is revealed. All the attributes of appearance and functions of the body are in reality the essence of body? A life like statue of yours merely reveals the essence of sand or stone of which it is made.

Nature of Soul

Otherwise it merely feeds one's imagination. The revealed nature or essence or soul of the body is in the wholeness of its existence? It is like the sense of presence of current in an electric wire. There is sensation of presence of electricity in the live wire. The same sensation is absent in the non-live wire.

Soul is the eternal presence of your body. It is the presence of awareness in self & others, both internal and external. Is this presence different in every creature? Does my soul is different from that of yours?

Soul is not individual or personal. It is the soul of the whole body of organisms. One organism may die. Its organizing molecules lose integration. It becomes part of chemical matter. But the bigger body of organisms is still there. When you see a settlement of ants you see the whole colony not individual ants. You don't name individual ants. When you see a single bacterium under microscope you actually visualize its specie. The whole colony of this specie is there on the germinating media. You only select one to study its physical features.

Life is the presence of internal awareness in all organisms; it does lay bare the presence of soul in whole body organism.

So it is not the question of one soul present in individual body. It is the soul of humanity in all humans or soul of creation in all creation or soul of universe in whole of universe. When you individualize it is the same soul manifesting. This soul gets individualized but is not personalized. In a group this individuation fades away. When an individual creation dies away it dies fully, it does not leave behind soul. Soul is not personal. Personal elements in us are ego and mind which are born with body and die with it. There is no universal abode of departed souls. This single fact if understood and realized properly decides our complete liberation after death.

Soul is the life in the matter. When an individual creation dies away it dies fully. It leaves behind disarranged matter; it does not leave behind soul. It simply stops short of life individually in scientific sense. But at the same time life or say soul is present in other creations.

One bacterium divides into many. After every division it produced new offspring bacteria. When it was aged and lost strength, it was going to die. It chose a mode of survival in the form of division and producing offspring bacteria. Now can we ask where now the original bacterium is? Where is its dead body? A colony of bacteria there by produced may have started from one single bacterium. Whole of creation may have started from one seed of life. This seed of life as soul of life started living in many. In single bacterium it manifests as individual soul but it is not personal soul of that bacterium! Same is true of other creation.

Soul is not personal. The soul is not one's personalized possession. Individual elements in us are mind or ego. They are personalized and worldly. They separate one from the rest of world. These elements came into existence after the original consciousness reflected over itself after birth and they are born in the world. A child in the womb is part of mother both as body and psyche. It feels what the mother feels. After birth child is exposed to multiple relation with the world. It react with outer and creates his individual feelings. This whole set of his individual reactions makes him individual. This makes his personality. This makes his ego.

We feel individuation because of the presence of this mind or ego in us. Soul is not individual, soul is not personal. Yes we tend to live after death. It is only by way of producing progeny or offspring. Nature from its very inception was harsh to the living forms. So the life forms chose that mode of survival. There is genetic continuity of life and organism tends to live after death as the offspring. This is discussed in other pages of this book.

The soul is the reality, the real nature of the body. Like essence of a flower it emanates through its sensation. It is revealed from the way the body exhibits itself; the way body presents itself to others. The way the body creates whole physical, emotional or sensational field around itself.

The soul is the reality, is the real nature of the body. It is not something existing as philosophical thought, understood by intellectual part of brain. It is not the deduction or logic. It is not the understanding. It is real and perceptible! It is the awareness. Revealed to you through fine or still finer perception! Soul is revealed to all the creatures even to those who may or may not have intellectual functions.

Does this soul present only in living creatures, in life forms? Is it not there an abundant matter in the universe which is not live in strict biological sense? The universe is a substance. This universe with myriad of planets, stars and black holes; the whole atomic and sub atomic realities, whole magnetism, electricity, light and sound is not mere a physical field;

without any inherent essence; without any inherent soul, without any inherent awareness!

In same way as human soul, the soul of universe is not something hidden, hidden behind matter or away from matter! The planets and black hole does not hide but reveals their soul; the universal soul? It is revealed by their function, by the arrangement, by their de-arrangement and by rearrangement. By the cycle of birth and death of stars and galaxies! Yes physical laws do exist both in live and non live forms. Universal soul is the eternal presence of 'essence of universe' in all heavenly bodies. In human body this eternal presence manifest as awareness, awareness of matter. In universe this eternal presence manifest as awareness of the universe. Our miniscule material body, miniscule intelligence, miniscule awareness cannot comprehend this internal awareness of universe. This just as we on earth cannot feel the speed with which the earth moves.

This soul of the universe is the universal soul existing as the Reality of universe. All the attributes of appearance of the universe are not hiding its soul; they are revealing it. The outward appearance and functional presence of universe reveals the eternal and infinite essence of the universe.

The real nature of universe, its essence or its soul does not exist as a separate entity, as an intervening third party or to say as God or Reality existing away or beyond its body of planets and stars, atoms and molecules. There must not be some God existing as separate entity from rest of universe, some anthropomorphic God, chemical or sub-atomic God, as particle or energy separate from particles or energy of universe. Or existing as someone hidden behind the veil of his existence or any other individual creation? Or some philosophically deduced God! It is all utterly absurd and inconceivable.

Reality is the attribute, the feature, the property, the quality, the trait, the sensation, the feeling of the universe as a substance. Just close your eyes and you know you are not alone; there exists the universe and you feel its vibrations. Existent universe is the face of the reality. As you go into the depth of universe you find so many deeper layers of reality.

Universe exists both as a seed and full bloomed expanding universe. That is its life and death; the death being start of new life. Universe before big bang is the seed of universe. The same seed would go dormant after its contraction, the big crunch! Universal soul or Brham' (Skt.-the ever expanding universe literally!) is the names of same reality, a symbolic representation by words. Before we name anything we create a totality of that first. Then we select a symbolic word best suitable to this totality. A symbolic word or name or appellation is merely revealed in the mind and conveys the comprehensible meaning of things we observe. A crow is a crow because it crows. Name is not the reality. If you yourself crow you don't become crow. Naming the things is all rational comprehension. Names points out towards the reality.

God is not hidden

God is natured in nature   Swaran J.
(03-04-14)

Reality of universe is both submerged and revealed nature of nature i.e. nature of its body.

God is natured in nature. God is not hidden from nature. God is not away from nature.

Every spec of creation, its chemical or physical part; its atomic or sub-atomic division reveals the soul or nature of God, or the universe. Material existence does not hide nature, rather reveals it. For the time till we devise physical methods to know the presence of inherent nature we deduce them as philosophical or mathematical truths. The logic seems hard and theoretical at first but becomes obvious and observable as you gain more and more internal vision.

God is both substance and nature of the substance. No energy or particle as different or secret as Higgs or God particle exist differently or separate from whole. God as substance is utterly indivisible and exists as the one whole substance. All matter, the dark matter, the anti matter or whatever comprehended or discovered so far exist as one substance. All the quanta, the waves, the particles denote the same substance. No independent existence of separate substance from the main can be conceived. Behind the apparent multiplicity there is one single unity. Whole is one single whole not otherwise. This as totality is one single substance that makes nature. No other matter different from whole matter of universe exists. All individual elements are but a form of energy manifesting to join or bond each other to chemical and physical manifestations. The chemical bonding in a particular way create biological life and life forms.

This single substance pervades and invades the nature. This does not evade the nature.

God is both the function and reality of this substance, of the gross nature. God as nature acts from the same necessity by which it exists. It is infinite, necessary, uncaused and indivisible reality. This one single substance is infinite. No other substance which is other than this can be the cause of it. No God separate from his own nature can be conceived. Hence realty as we name it as God is Uncaused. Cause will come if another substance exists parallel to universe.

Manifest nature is extended in its qualities. Extension is another attribute of the God. God as substance is extended in its properties. Biological matter is extension of chemical and physical matter. Mind and thoughts are the extensions of the biological matter. Mind of man is the extension of the physical body. Thoughts and ideas are the extensions of mind. Intellectuality and wisdom are extensions of thoughts. They all stem from single substance which is matter in exact physical sense.

Similarly man as body is extended substance of nature and man as mind is an extended substance of universal mind. Everything in extension has the same physical continuation as of the primary matter. The soul, the consciousness, God or spirit are the physical attributes though these things are not quantifiable by known physical methods. But this does not mean that they are imagined. Imagination is constructed by the thoughts to make understandable themes. Imagination as an act is physical attribute of mind but something which is imagined by the thoughts but has no physical existence is not part of nature. So any idea which arises in the mind is just one mode or attribute of nature of God. It is not mere expression of the attribute, it is the attribute. Something that exists in nature and idea of that something which exists in mind belong to same substance. Infinite series of ideas arising in human minds constitute God's mind or infinite intellect of the nature.

Matter is both live and non-live. All matter exists as necessity of existence. Both lion and cow have their own necessities. Matter does not judge the matter. Does not put bars to the choices. Matter is randomly free though act strictly to the physico-chemical laws that have been evolved and still evolving. These laws are not planned or devised. A judging God who has plans and act purposefully is not the real God or soul of nature. Nature doesn't judge what her creatures do! God do not judge or punish his creation. God of one's own thoughts, an imaginary one is not the real God. Seeing God as one who is to be pacified through prayers is absurd and inconceivable.

As nature or God or universe has no definite cause so they have no definite end. It begins from where it ends and still not cyclic. It is astonishingly evolutionary. There are no plans or goals of nature. Nature is not necessarily pre-determined. So God or soul of nature cannot not pre-plan everything or put higher creation as man to be part of their plans. The things follow one another without any conceivable predestined end or predetermined origin. This one single attribute determines freedom of man on earth.

All revealed religions reveal mind of universe. They merely unmask the universal laws of existence. A creation such as man is bound to limit his vision to see the exact reality of universal laws. All beliefs in conscience, morality, love, faith in God etc. are not mere concepts created by man. They are revealed laws of nature. They are created for peaceful co-existence and avoid undue devastation.

Nature by its own exists in same two modes. It creates balance in the form of peaceful co-existence for creation but still everything can be destroyed in seconds for the purpose of random recreation. It is all random. To escape from this chance randomness we create well structured psychological and imagined God. This is simply invented to create a life of order to escape random destruction and to have sufficient mental freedom to look for other intelligent aspects of nature. These psychological principles do not exist in the physical world and only cause a small negligible change of physical world. Exact physical world exists independently of psychology of the higher creation like men.

— 0 —

(6)

The Great Grip of Knowledge-
(Great obstacle to Freedom)

We are in grip of ideas and thoughts. **We are in the grip of knowledge.** We are in grip of ever burdening information about Self, God, this and that. All these no doubt give us a nice pastime and have become our pleasurable pursuit.

The grip is that of sudden conclusions which arrives in our mind and doesn't leave us free for other alternative thoughts to look for.

Conclusions are thought activity in the mind which is conditioned with the past knowledge. These conclusions are references of our previous knowledge.

We are souls defragmented from great sea of existence and suddenly became aware of our own individual existence. We also suddenly came to know what surrounds us. We are surrounded by similar creatures like us. But can we appreciate the air which immediately surrounds us. Can we appreciate it visually? In the great sea of existence we never knew what we are surrounded by.

You liked that story of young fish who one day asked her mother fish, "Where is that sea I often hear about?"

"O fool this is what surrounds you?"

So this baby fish is completely immersed in the great sea of existence. She is aware of her existence only and as that of other creatures of sea. But what about the sea that surrounds her. This mother fish may have been once out of sea and then again back. She now knows the importance of sea. She now is aware of her individual existence. She has grown in her a little "self" who can distinguish her from the outer whole, the sea.

This self awareness can't let her to immerse back in the sea same way as the baby fish she herself had been. She can't lose awareness of self though knowing fully that great sea of existence surrounds it. This is highest paradox. We know the sea of existence as our abode but can't get back into it without our little self. This self creates for her so conspicuous an existence that she now exists separate from rest of the sea. Self creates individuality. Baby fish does not know that she exists separate from the sea. She doesn't know even that there is sea. She is free from her individual burden of existence.

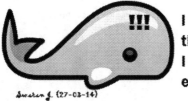

!!! I fail to see the sea which I hear from every other!!

Swaran J. (27-03-14)

Mother fish was free before all the knowledge of sea came into her mind.

This self awareness is the start of her own little knowledge of "Self and the Sea." She was there in the sea, happy and playful with other creatures but she was unaware that she is different and away. Once this knowledge strikes that she has a separate and contingent existence, it adds to her horror.

This knowledge of separation is her little grip that keeps her away from her once complete immersion in the sea. She is struggling to be free from this grip but knowing not how to be.

We collect more ideas and information and refine it to more and more knowledge to get individual freedom but little knowing how to overcome separation and contingency of human existence.

This grip of knowledge is the tight hold of our collected information. This tight hold is all that adds to our being self conscious. Like a little chap who can't recite fully learned nursery rhyme because of being conscious among the surrounding elders.

We are behaving as out of ocean even while in ocean; ocean of the universal existence, our collective existence.

Man does live in this ocean but has carved a personal boundary out of collective existence. This personal boundary is boundary of physical space he carries with his frail body. Or it is inner space he carries with his confused mind. Or there it is spiritual space he carries in form of his fixed ideas and opinion, even his personal God and personal guru.

This is all nothing but his overused and confused mind. Everyone out there all guides like mother fish instructs him the 'phony' ways to attain freedom, to reach Nirvana—or liberation[11].

All the personal boundaries of ours are personal hell. One needs to cross them before crossing over to the sea of Nirvana. One does not need to learn knowledge of nirvana; one only needs to de-learn knowledge of separation.

In the forward journey of the soul to end the separation it fails her to observe effectively the field of her moves. It de-potentiates her resolve and then in the real grip of knowledge she talks no more of freedom. She talks no more of the freedom of action; talks no more to go into the unfamiliar once again. She now moves in the known fields. The known field gives her security of existence. The grip of known field becomes tighter. There begins a dread to move out of known existence.

This de-learning of knowledge of separation is not all easy. Here one does not need some resolve on the part of mind. All such resolves will add up to more separation. One perhaps needs an unbroken non-personal immersion into sea of existence.

Original abode of soul is not something out there. It is very much here. It is like going into childhood state when you

---

[11]   Nirvāṇa (Sanskrit) literally means "blown out", as in a candle. It is most commonly associated with Buddhism. In Indian religions, the attainment of nirvana is *moksha* i.e. liberation from the cycle of rebirth.

did not have personal boundaries. To search the unknown as original abode we are not to begin our journey by searching guides. We have simply lost this knowledge that our original abode is the same sea of existence which surrounds us but our becoming "self conscious" forbade us to have that complete immersion.

This playful abode of souls, the sea of existence is not something that exists in heaven. It exists around each one of us. But only the 'separated self' does not allow us to absorb in it completely. If ever it happens we will be completely free. The hell of separation, the real bondage of self will be gone forever.

The freedom is a buzz word in the world today. We talk too much about it. We have given it too much importance.

Don't we ever wonder! What is biologically available to us for example the body—why it should be obstacle to liberation? What is available to us mentally i.e. the mind, knowledge, thoughts why they should obstruct our freedom? What is available to us spiritually i.e. the soul, the spirit, or God— they should be liberated always, already, before even we have any thought of freedom.

Only not liberated is our thought. Only not liberated is our mind who carry the thought. Only not liberated is the 'self' which is separated from our universal sea of existence.

We must not give so much importance to the thought and mental space it carries. If it is engaged in the world the way it feels so—separated or otherwise why should we bother? There exist many a things in us which are universally immersed in the sea of existence. Such elements in us don't need any "noisy" liberation.

Why to be so much after salvation part, knowing that we are already liberated.

Just consider if you had never come across the word 'freedom' in your life; if you had never understood it in the mind; if you had never realized that it is so important, the way it was put before you by the academic world.

Just consider if you were always life's slave; slave of totality; slave of reality; carrying God's deeper designs, never knowing what they are—you were always free. You were free from the thoughts of freedom. You were always free from the "separated little self" grown out of proportion to a "big fat ego" in this world.

The same thing must we understand now. We are known to this freedom as a word. But look, there may be some better word, having some better meanings, a better engagement of us in the world! There may be some better realization of it. There may be some better theme than this 'liberation'; which we have not known still; nature's deeper design; a deeper gift for us being here in the world. Why do we want to have the knowledge of it to carry it forward? To carry forward it knowingly and schematically! Or academically!! Why should we again make it obsolete like this much abused word freedom? Let the charm of having it without our 'knowledge' remains!

We are what we are. If we deem liberated we are so. If not we are not. There is one great force inside us called 'our mind'. It is so because we rarely understand the way how we use mind; whether it is we who are using the mind or it the mind who uses us; whether we tell the mind to have one particular thought or mind tells us to accept the thoughts it carries.

How you take the things, is the tip.

— 0 —

(7)

Reflection over Consciousness
(Precognitive Perception)

What is consciousness and what do we mean by reflection over consciousness?

Idea of consciousness is quite primitive one but the modern concept of consciousness started taking shape at least during late seventeenth century when John Locke described it in one of his essays.

Meaning awareness literally, it is also termed as subjective experience or sense of selfhood. It also means wakefulness when it is differentiated from sleep or unconsciousness. An anesthetized person looses consciousness hence it is synonymous with aesthesis which means awareness of the senses.

Though all cells of body are conscious but nervous and sensory apparatus of the body carry perceptive consciousness. Consciousness appears to lie in nervous system, our brain, spinal cord along with senses like—vision, hearing, taste, smell and touch and pain. These are input and output devices while central brain is the processing apparatus.

All these senses perceive environment as sensors and act as transducers. This means that they have ability to change environmental energy of sound, light etc. into electrical energy in the nervous cells. Cells are both conscious to this electrical energy and respond accordingly and also to certain chemicals called neurotransmitters. Other cells in the body are conscious to other circulating chemicals e.g. hormones, oxygen, carbon dioxide and ultimately all these tissues respond as the body.

A great body of philosophical work on consciousness has been done by philosophers since time immemorial like Kant[12], Husserl[13], Heidegger[14], Sartre[15], and William

---

[12] **Immanuel Kant (1724-1804)** is one of the most influential philosophers in the history of Western philosophy. His contributions to metaphysics, epistemology, ethics, and aesthetics have had a profound impact on almost every philosophical movement that followed him.

[13] **Edmund Husserl (1859-1938),** is the "father" of the philosophical movement known as phenomenology. Phenomenology can be roughly described as the sustained attempt to describe experiences (and the "things themselves") without metaphysical and theoretical speculations.

[14] **Martin Heidegger (1889-1976)** is widely acknowledged to be one of the most original and important philosophers of the 20th century. Heidegger's main interest was ontology or the study of being. In his fundamental treatise, *Being and Time*, he attempted to access being (Sein) by means of phenomenological analysis of human existence (Dasein) in respect to its temporal and historical character.

[15] **Jean Paul Sartre (1905-1980):** His philosophical career of focuses, in its first phase, upon the construction of a philosophy of existence known as existentialism.

James[16] just to name a few. A parallel work have been done by quantum physicists like Bohr[17], Heisenberg[18], Schrodinger[19], who gave the shape to the quantum concept of consciousness and today's scientists theorists like Ken Wilber[20] are continuing to explain new concepts of consciousness.

---

[16] **William James (1842-1910)** is considered by many to be the most insightful and stimulating of American philosophers. His contributions in these areas included critiques of long-standing philosophical positions on such issues as freedom vs. determinism, correspondence vs. coherence, and dualism vs. materialism, as well as a thorough analysis of a phenomenological understanding of the self and consciousness, a "forward-looking" conception of truth (based on validation and revisable experience).

[17] **Niels Henrik David Bohr** (1885-1962) was a Danish physicist who made foundational contributions to understanding Atomic and quantum theory, for which he received the Nobel prize in Physics in 1922. Bohr was also a philosopher and a promoter of scientific research.

[18] **Werner Karl Heisenberg** (1901-1976) was a German theoretical physicist and one of the key creators of quantum mechanics. His famous **Heisenberg's Uncertainty principle** ascribes the uncertainty in the measurable quantities to the jolt-like disturbance triggered by the act of observation.

[19] **Erwin Rudolf Josef Alexander Schrödinger** (1887-1961) was a Nobel Prize-winning Austrian physicist who developed a number of fundamental results in the field of quantum theory, which formed the basis of wave mechanics.

[20] **Kenneth Earl "Ken" Wilber II** (b.1949) is an American writer and public speaker. He has written and lectured about mysticism, philosophy, ecology and development psychology. His work formulates what he calls Integral Theory. In 1998 he founded the Integral Institute.

These scientists did strive to find the exact nature of conscious experience in the brain. Some put the center of this experience somewhere in the Limbic system or pineal gland. This can be termed a pointless approach to the study of consciousness and this much is certain that whole of our brain and nervous system and hormonal activity act jointly to produce conscious experience?

Why do we have this conscious experience? What is the scientific basis of consciousness? A great scientific body, current and preceding is devoted to this aspect of consciousness. But for present our theme of this book is not to reproduce or explain this work or propose some new opinion.

Whatsoever may be the physical, physiological or chemical basis of our consciousness we can simply say that we are conscious and aware because of consciousness? Right from lowest unicellular organism to the highest creation i.e. man all are conscious thus having faculty of consciousness. While all other lower animals are simply conscious of the outer environment and can perceive weather or danger etc. But man is perhaps single animal conscious of his own perceptions.

This faculty of being conscious of one's own consciousness will be called faculty of reflection. This ability to reflect is not new but quite primitive ever since man gained awareness of his acts and motives in the world. From the Neanderthal, Denisova & Hominin man[21] we moved on the

---

[21] **Neanderthal, Denisova & hominin man and *Homo sapiens H. neanderthalensis***, alternatively designated as ***Homo sapiens neanderthalensis***, lived in Europe and Asia from 400,000 to about 30,000 years ago. **Denisovans** belonged

evolutionary ladder to be *Homo sapiens* and became highest creature on earth to have wisdom of self and surrounding environment. By sapience it is meant to be wisdom of man because of his self consciousness & thinking ability. It is the ability to think and act utilizing knowledge, experience, understanding, common sense and insight—so states the Collins Dictionary regarding meaning of sapience.

This original ability of gathering and utilizing information is of the consciousness which is the state of being aware. Because of the consciousness we have the ability to perceive the environment and also the ability to reflect over our perceptions.

Reflection is a great thing. This faculty leads us to self knowledge, making us knower of our being. The pioneers of oriental philosophy became aware of this faculty in quite earlier days of the advent of civilization. That is why books like Vedas, Holy Gita, and Upanishads carry abundance of material which was not merely the product of man's interaction with outer environment i.e. objective knowledge but his reflections on his consciousness activity i.e. subjective knowledge.

---

to the same lineage as Neanderthals, with the two diverging shortly after their line split from that lineage giving rise to modern humans. **Hominidae** (great apes) speciated from the ancestors of the **gibbon** (lesser apes).

Archaic *Homo sapiens* the forerunner of anatomically modern humans, evolved between 400,000 and 250,000 years ago.

Source; http://en.wikipedia.org/wiki/Human_evolution#Neanderthal_and_Denisova_hominin

All contemplating activities over the past foregone acts, analyzing their meaning, drawing conclusions, putting them in categories, using them as references, weighing future actions in the light of previous ones, are our prime reflections. All our writings, poetry, singing, dancing, painting, drama are one or other form of reflection.

We gather knowledge, solve problems, grow intellectually and become wise through reflection. Such reflections are needed certainly for the development of the civic world where humans make mistakes and execute the corrections. The marvelous development of the world is the result of our continuous reflection over the blunders.

These reflections carrying conclusions and corrections have very little to do for development & manifestation of the consciousness. The evolution of consciousness comes only when there is real change from primitive hostile animal reactions and understanding larger aspects of human existence.

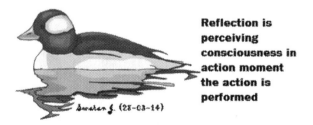

Reflection is perceiving consciousness in action moment the action is performed

Performance of an activity is an act of consciousness. We have seen in the previous chapters that we always react to something and perhaps never acted of our own. The origin of action we mistakenly believe is from us but action is actually created by our immediate environment which put before us a challenge and we create solution to our needs and desires.

There is not only the environment outside the body but there is similar environment inside the body. French Physiologist Claude Bernard[22] called it the 'milieu interior' or internal environment of the body. Consciousness is aware of both. We react to both of them. A less quantity of body water in the body is perceived as thirst and we not only perceive this but also carry forward the action by taking enough water. Any such change in the environment is perceived as shift from normal and body's feedback systems strive to redo this shift. Environment includes other creatures like us and we sometime react to our collective needs.

We react to our bodily needs e.g. hunger or thirst or pain and find their solution in the environment. We react to the forces of the nature to save ourselves or to the challenges posed by others. We react only and we may not find a single instance where we have not reacted but acted otherwise. We may not be able to find a single action which we can term as pure action. We can term an action as original and pure if it is emerging out of our free will and not from our reactive will. We are bound to follow every single reaction we make and create an endless chain of consequences. With small effort we can even predict a reaction in a person to life situations.

---

[22] **Claude Bernard (1813-1878)** was a French Physiologist. Among many other accomplishments, he was one of the first to suggest the use of blind experiments to ensure the objectivity of scientific observations. He was the first to define the term milieu interieur, now known as homeostasis. Source: http://en.wikipedia.org/wiki/Claude_Bernard

An action is original and pure and free only if it has the quality to complete itself—i.e. chosen, done and forgotten with no visible consequences. But a person carries consequences of his acts does not become free from them. He carries them during whole of his life. Even some of these consequences are shifted to his progeny then to theirs and so on. He is bound to his actions till his last day. He is programmed like a computer to re-act to his current and past actions and reactions.

So he is pre-programmed to respond and carry forward not only the consequences of his immediate actions but also the actions of the past. I may call my sitting on the computer; calling my action of writing for readers as action of my free will. I may call this my original action! But my conception is entirely wrong. Going back, if I recapitulate what in my life compelled me to take up my present action and what compelled this previous one and I contemplate so on so forth, *ad infinitum*, I find that it was all due to endless chain of reactions and I am bound to carry this chain, bound to carry consequences.

At the time of performance of action, the consciousness is as busy as anything and all the physical and mental faculties of our body have come into play. Imagine a soldier in action at the border or a scientist in his laboratory. He is not deliberately seeing himself performing an action. Only in later moments when war is over, he narrates his story he sees himself exactly in the same scene and can recount the minor details. But at the exact moment we cannot deliberately see ourselves performing action.

So we can either perform the action or see ourselves performing the action—we cannot perform both activities at the same time.

We can either taste the food or perceive ourselves tasting the food, not both. The same is true of other senses and sensory phenomenon. Once a particular action has been carried out to its effectiveness we come to know the quality of our performance. We have either spilled the ink or milk or entered a wrong key on the keyboard!

Can we perform both the activities at the same time—performing the action and seeing ourselves performing the action? That perhaps is what to say of reflection. This can be done when action is minimal or during meditative stage when outer action is just negligible.

While reflecting over our own self during meditative state, it seems to us that movement of our act is from outer to inner. It seems to us that as we close our eyes, whole of the external world is taken away from the senses and we are one with the feeling of our body, then of breathing, of digestive movements, then with our mind and our thoughts.

All our emotions, our desires and frustrations come right behind our eyes and we can feel them creating ruckus on our mental stage. We can see our sadness or happiness grow when we are away from external world. If we keep on visualizing ourselves internally for some period, we no longer tolerate to sustain our concentration and try to stand up immediately and get involve with the outer world.

This simple instance of momentary closing our eyes further strengthens our belief that there is an external world and there is internal world. Or there is an exterior and interior of our existence. But this is a mere belief and in the real sense this is not true. We have created so much indulgence with the world outside that it seems imperative that inner world exists separately from the outer.

In the real sense the existence that we speak of is not divided into exterior or interior. To relate with the exterior it is the consciousness which does so whom we deem interior of our body. Inner is always joining the outer during any performance.

When I talk I immediately visualize myself speaking from some inner core. It not only appears so but is true also that I reside in this inner core. When I move from this core I had to first cross my own body to reach to next body, person or object. But my inner core is continuously revealed to the outer in the form of my speech and body language.

In the long run we shall see that all these objects including my own body seem disconnected from each other as long as I maintain (my) exterior and interior. As an observer I have trained my eyes and discerning mind to observe myself away or separate from the observed things. This separation and further naming & categorization of objects seems helping me to interact with the world.

Descartes[23] while trying to prove his inner essence or the consciousness said, which is his now famous dictum, *cogito*

---

[23] **René Descartes (1596-1650)** was French mathematician, philosopher, and physiologist. From him we owe the first systematic account of the mind/body relationship. "If we wish our science to be complete, those matters which promote the end we have in view must one and all be scrutinized by a movement of thought which is continuous and nowhere

ergo sum, which means, I think, therefore I am (existing). He
wanted to assert that thinking is the main act of consciousness.
If I want to prove my own existence then the first thing that
comes for my shelter is the thinking i.e. I have a thought of
me. No dead matter will be having faculty of thinking. It
appears to me that I am thinking, or I have a 'thinking self'
which thinks for me. Or you can say it as 'I reside in my
thought'. Then it can be proved that consciousness in me exists
and I am that thinking because of consciousness. It may also
seem that consciousness is thinking for me separately from me!

"But immediately I noticed that while I was trying thus
to think everything false it was necessary that I, who was
thinking this was something. And observing that this truth,
"I am thinking therefore I exist," was so firm and sure
that all the most extravagant suppositions of the skeptics
were incapable of shaking it, I decided that I could accept
it without scruple as the first principle of the philosophy I
was seeking," Descartes wrote in his most quoted treatise
Discourse on Method (Part IV) in 1637.

But thinkers next in the line like Sartre deny that. For
him this is not true. The consciousness is not the thinking
body. It is the state or faculty of awareness which makes the
individual as 'conscious being' and makes him aware of the
environment. When we think there is another activity of
this consciousness. Thinking is the secondary activity of this
primary consciousness. Primarily consciousness is non-thinking

interrupted; they must also be included in an enumeration
which is both adequate and methodical", he writes in "Rules
for the direction of the mind". Source: http://en.wikipedia.
org/wiki/Rules_for_the_Direction_of_the_Mind

consciousness. Sartre calls it "Pre-reflective Cogito". Being aware is the one and most important attribute of this consciousness.

Actually the Cartesian dictum according to Sartre should be, 'I am aware that I think therefore I am'. Consciousness with its own peculiar act of reflection reflects over itself. By doing so right since birth it has created a thinking body, the mind. Mind is not only the thinking part but also acts as executive while dealing with the civic world. So the mind is our Thinking Self. It creates and analyses thought. This thinking self can be termed 'Cartesian Cogito' in philosophy. Thus reflection is the main activity which joins thinking self with the consciousness and this activity of reflection needs our further considerations.

Consciousness is one single straight forward action of the universe with continuity since infinity. Redoing and correcting activity only pertains to mind of man who wants to live in an unsullied and orderly civic world. All such corrections are all bindings to original act of consciousness and create burden upon already burdened consciousness. For consciousness every doing is an act that may be right or wrong. How and why do we categorize our doing as mistakes or correct doings is the act of analytic mind? Consciousness is the aware state of the body. This awareness becomes divided if we perform multiple tasks. You make mistakes when you have multiple jobs at hand.

So consciousness is burdened by mind, the thinking part of us. We live in world with a curse of doing multiplicity of actions with multiplicity of consequences. Only if this burden is not there, consciousness is free, fully aware.

— 0 —

(8)

Mind of the Consciousness
(How Consciousness Creates Mind?)

Mind is the function of both egoistic and non-egoistic activities of consciousness. Egoistic activities are all personal and non-egoistic merely subconscious and impersonal. For creation of ego, consciousness has to move self reflectively in the world which means knowing about herself and her relationship with the world.

We are born with the wonderful, self-illuminating essence of creation i.e. consciousness. Consciousness at the time of birth is in its original state of being, having all the movements of perception i.e. feeling and sensing the things but with very little reflection over its activities. The moment child tastes anything, milk or honey, he is exposed to another activity of consciousness which can be seen as "reflection" over activity or "reflection of tasting sweet". It feels good so taste is the first perception of the world we get after taking birth. (And lifelong we are obsessed with this sensation!)

Perception of taste is the first reflection of the consciousness by which she felt satisfaction after exhausting herself because of continuous crying and being in an unfamiliar environment. If next experience is somewhat painful it gets recorded too. In this way it is exposed to pleasure and pain with categorization right since birth.

Mind is the name of functional activity of consciousness by with it perceives the world and stores these perceptions as knowledge and memory.

This activity of mind leads us to the faculty of thinking, the process of making and developing thoughts. A thought is a cyclic change of appearing and disappearing neurotransmitter in a particular group of neurons. They start firing when a particular stimulus activates one of them. After sufficient repetition of same thought it gets conditioned to appear or disappear at regular intervals or whenever stimulus is there. A person so conditioned becomes a victim of tyranny of thoughts. Excessive indulgence in the process of thinking causes the consciousness work slowly. By burdening her with both inner and outer activity we lose a part of our awareness. A person standing at the sentry post does not indulge in thought activity. He remains simply aware without making his own thoughts and executing them.

With time we create a sufficiently capable mind which can shut and start our transaction with the world the same way a PC window does. With mind we know both the outer activity and inner thoughts. Mind is thus software, an autopilot which exists outside consciousness and joins her with the world. Without mind, consciousness will never know that there is a world and without mind again, we shall never know there is consciousness. Akin to the window software of a computer, it separates the individual consciousness from the world and thus creates the sense of separation from the outer.

Absence of mind means 'window crash' as seen in mental disorders where person do not know his entity lose insight for example in certain mental disorders like Schizophrenia, depression etc. So without mind we cannot move an inch in the world. But mind should always remain as function. It should not turn into an entity. It should not show his presence. Like it shows when it is burdened or pre-occupied. Here in that case absence of mind also means Faster Window. Memory is not always the stored memory, the hard disc, knowledge collected by mind. Memory is working memory too, i.e. the RAM[24] (random access memory of computer). It is there when you have enough empty space in the brain. When neurons are receptive to every new encounter or information! This empty space is created by meditation. During meditation you clean your hard disc (brain) of unwanted information. You compartmentalize the previously stored information readily accessible files and folders. You create enough empty space for new information.

Right from birth a person involves himself with his immediate environment, people around him. He categorizes not only the things outside world but also the effects or

---

[24] **RAM** is an acronym for *random access memory*, a type of computer memory that can be accessed randomly; that is, any byte of memory can be accessed without touching the preceding bytes. RAM is the most common type of memory found in computers. Source: http://www.webopedia.com/TERM/R/RAM.html

impressions these things create. He also at one point of time sees both the world and himself at the same time.

He sees himself in the light of others. He starts having anxiety of performance. He starts getting praise or rebuke from others. He creates a little niche of himself in his own mind. In that slot he makes an image of himself. In the start this image is fluidic or changes daily. But afterwards it gets solidified and person permanently starts having a distinct personality of his own. He is conditioned with his own thoughts about him and so is his behavior with the world. Consciousness doesn't bother about the world, way she look like, way she behaves, what others say about her etc. which means if consciousness does not become 'self-conscious', ego will not be created.

Mind is the window software of the brain!

Simple naive fellows who move non-reflectively in the world have less ego activity. Mind, the functional part of consciousness works both for ego and consciousness. Egoistic mind is the mind which takes active conscious part in this world in terms of gathering information and knowledge and interpreting and storing it for future use and having strong personal taint. Non-egoistic mind is subconscious or unconscious mind which functions without our knowing. It is a universal mind. We have similarity with every person in the world because of this universal mind and we act and react as everyone does.

Certain reactions are our universal reactions thus coming from our universal mind. A person trained in the discipline of Psychology or Psychiatry is able to deal with every human in any part of the world. As a universal mind we are one.

Consciousness we are born with is "pre-reflective cogito"[25]. This cogito or Consciousness is preliminary to the process of reflection. It is the 'Being-in-itself'. Reflection as activity of consciousness was executed after birth during engagement with the world. As primary consciousness one is simply conscious without having consciousness of consciousness i.e. reflection over consciousness. When one is simply conscious one cannot explain or declare what does one perceives. At this state there is awareness but no awareness of awareness. There is attention without self attention. It is an animal awareness, purely biological, purely forward not reflected over itself.

Once consciousness become aware of its being i.e. 'Being-in-itself' it becomes self aware. Self aware consciousness is 'Being-for-itself', as says Sartre. Consciousness does so by reflection. It reflects over its own activities. It starts moving in

---

[25] **Pre-reflective self-consciousness** is pre-reflective in the sense that it is an awareness we have before we do any reflecting on our experience;) it is an implicit and first-order awareness rather than an explicit or higher-order form of self-consciousness

time and space it creates an 'executive self' in the form of ego by which it will be known to the world. Ego is an imitation of consciousness. It comes into the world by continuous 'reflection activity' of consciousness. It is also not going to remain after death.

Process of development of ego is process of creation of structuralized boundaries within the infinite nature of consciousness. On one side it has structural boundary with the world from which it is protected and which restricts its freedom of action in the formal civic world. And on other side it hampers this primary consciousness from entering into its unknown depths right up to the centrality of the universe. Ego is our personal boundary of which we are conscious and it will always remain in the world at the objective pole of consciousness. This means consciousness is pure subject and exists as 'pure me' and one can see the ego, as executive personality in the same way one sees other personalities of the world.

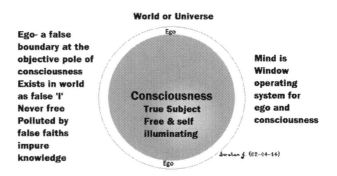

What Descartes was trying to prove by his dictum, *cogito ergo sum* was not the consciousness but the existence of thinking self in the body. This is the self which we usually refer as 'I' while in the world, this 'I' is not our actual 'I'. Ego as 'I' is a permanent vestige in the consciousness and mind is the running software for the consciousness. Both exist in the world, same way as other persons and objects. They create a psychic reality in the world we live as opposed to physical reality which is as the world is. Psychic reality is born and dies with us while physical reality is there whether we are in the world or not.

— 0 —

(9)

Unity of World and Mind
(Our Psychic and Physical Reality)

The objects we see outside, in the world, in this universe are physical ones. Physical pertains to matter. Everything is matter so says Physics and exist as the solids, liquids, gasses, inorganic matter (chemicals), organic matter (plants and animals), atoms, molecules, subatomic particles, protons, neutrons, electrons, energy, magnetism, light, electricity, gravity, gravitation etc. etc. all are forms of physical matter or their properties.

The consciousness the prime observer of all is a part of physical world and is not created or imagined by mind as a philosophical theme. As certain scientists believe consciousness do takes origin from matter & they call it an epiphenomenon of matter. Some others call it an emergent property of matter, in the language of science which emerges out of combination of the lower properties i.e. light, magnetism, electricity, and chemical binding and interactions.

This property of matter is to become conscious of itself comes after interactions of all physical properties in a particular system in a particular way. Human body, a plant or an animal body too, is that system. Biological Matter like bacteria and the evolved species to higher categories up to humans all are complex systems. Such systems are non-linear and many components of system act in complex ways. This leads to unpredictability of the behavior of the system.

All the physical matter is perceptible to consciousness. Consciousness is the prime developer of evolutionary changes in the brain or body of an organism. It creates gates of perception in the form of 'senses'. Our sensory organs like eye or ear are the modified cells. Both the stimulus and consciousness towards that stimulus act in cooperation for this modification. "An eye is created for the light by the light" so says Goethe.

When our human perceptions fail to perceive we take help of physical instruments like microscope or telescope, or MRI/CT scans etc. Whatever these physical instruments show they show facts of physical matter i.e. the micro features.

Everything we observe, perceive, measure or quantify comes in the preview of physics. The consciousness which itself is never measured or scrutinized with any physical instrument so far still a part of matter and an epiphenomenon of matter, scientists desperately want to prove. Like development of light or magnetism in the matter consciousness is similar mysterious development. So fasted it is bound to matter that we can't make it or think it separate it from the matter. It manifests when matter is so organized in a system as we see in biological organism be it plant or animal. It only goes into oblivion when biological matter is disorganized and not viable and is dead. It does not need proof of its existence because it is one which makes the biological matter aware to surroundings. In higher animals it creates a sense of "I" or "self" which is self-aware activity of consciousness.

Like consciousness mind or ego too are also not visible to the physical instruments. While dissecting body during surgical procedures do we ever see mind. But how can we objectify the consciousness to prove its presence? We already have the presence of it as observer. But man has devised the ways to objectify consciousness as well as the mind or psyche. As we study Psychology; we study the mind or psyche; we study thousands of its subsidiary branches; we can distinguish or diagnose normal or abnormal mind just as the physical body; still no psychologist can claim to know the physical presence of mind. Can we separate mind from the physical side of it, the body. But as stated earlier mind is the function and consciousness is state of awareness. How can we make both mind and consciousness 'the entity' and call for the proof of physical presence of these? Function of a machine is visible when machine is functioning.

But how this mind observes reality? How it gets and records the impressions? How these impressions so impress the mind that it gets related or attached to some? Mind observes and experiences. This experience of mind is not single but double. It is either psychic experience or physical experience. The psychic one is more personal. That is why mind gets involved with two worlds—the world of psychic objects and physical objects. While in world mind creates two distinguished categories of objects—physical and psychic. Physical objects are present in the world like house and roads, trees and mountains. Psychic objects are present in the mind and are created by mind.

Mind or human psyche has created for us a different sort of reality, the psychic reality. Objects in this psychic reality are in the same way as the physical ones. A person who is approaching me from a distance is a physical object and turns out to be my brother or sister or friend when comes near. Now he becomes a psychic object for me, someone related and present in me.

My wife before my marriage was woman for me like all other women of the world, a biological creature and physical objects to my observances. And once I was married to her she become part of my psychic reality, a psychic object. My children while playing in a group in school look like all other children to me, but once I recognize them they turn out to be my own children and to them I am more attached than other children of society.

My house, my shop, my area, my country all become forms of psychic objects when I put an adjective MY or MINE. I can distinguish even seeing their videos. Even the heavenly objects like sun, moon and Saturn etc. turn psychic when we observe them through our horoscope and infer their effect. Some of them are bad or evil *graha* (planets) while others are good and beneficial. Such effect is purely on our psyche as shown in the astrology books. If ever they affect physical side of us such effect is also through the mind or psyche. My photographs, my image, my strength and weakness are other vestiges of psychic reality existing in me.

None other than me is the creator of this psychic reality? Once I have validated this reality it becomes similarly harsh and cruel as the physical reality. A faraway house of a friend is a matter of physical stress for me while psychically placing this house as well as friend in my mind is cause of concern when he is in difficulty. Can I ever escape from this reality? My wife may leave me; my children may go away without ever caring me in my coming days even then they will never be the part of other physical objects to me. I will recognize them as mine even in the thick crowd. They will remain forever as my psychic objects.

I love certain people, and hate some others. Like I have grudges against certain people or affection towards others in the same way the whole of mankind, whole of humanity becomes psychic reality for me.

We make images of deity we adore or fear from. We adore even living persons, call them holy beings, make them living deities and put their images on the walls and seek salvation (from our psychic reality, perhaps!) by doing so. But do we ever imagine that we have made them even bigger a psychic reality. How would we seek deliverance from psychic reality by moving on to another psychic reality?

'Would you ever spit on the photograph (image) of your father', said Vivekananda[26] to a king who opposed image

---

[26] **Swami Vivekananda (1863-1902),** Bengal (India) born **Narendra Nath Datta** was an Indian Hindu monk and chief disciple of the 19th-century saint Ramakrishna. The context of story told here is as follows: When Narendra met the Mangal Singh, the king of Alwar, who was westernized in his outlooks. Singh asked Narendra questions and ridiculed Hindu idol worship. Narendra attempted to explain to him that that worship of the Hindus are symbolic worship, but failed to make the king understand. Then Narendra saw a painting hanging on the wall, it was the painting of the king's

worship. All images of gods and goddesses are our psychic reality and effect emanating from them is because of their effect on my mind. It is not direct physical effect as of light or sound. This effect becomes physical via the mind. It is a psychic effect.

There is a story of a prisoner who was pronounced penalty of death. He was to be given some poison which would kill him. He inhabited a cell where he was among many co-prisoners. A co-prisoner in the same cell who observed his execution was also to be poisoned in the coming days. When the exact day of his execution came he was not given poison but given similar but non-poisonous solution as a matter or experimentation by the executer. He died by the non-poisonous substance. This incidence tells us the extreme of psychic effect on the physical existence of body.

While in world mind creates two categories of objects-physical and psychic.

Swaran J. (28-03-14)

Is there any escape from this psychic reality?

deceased father and asked him to spit on it. Singh became angry and retorted how he could spit on his father. Narendra explained, though it was just a painting, not the king himself, it reminds everybody about the king, similarly an idol worshipped by a Hindu is actually a symbolic worship of the Supreme. Source: http://en.wikipedia.org/wiki/Vivekananda

Rama was another king like many rulers of Indian subcontinent, who happened to be pious, obedient and brave. But after his physical demise, his story was narrated so many times and now is the part of psychic reality of all devotional minds who worship him as their own savior, their god.

Our ego is the final unity in relation to all psychic objects of the world. Our consciousness is the final unity of all the physical objects. Consciousness is the physical observer of things while ego is the psychic observer. All the psychic objects are created by us. Physical objects are not created by us. Ego is the final perceiver of the psychic objects. Consciousness is the final perceiver of physical objects.

Once we have created psychic reality for ourselves there is no escape even in our dreams. When spirituality demands from us to end all attachments it actually demands that we should once again make all psychic objects as physical ones, remove the adjective MY or MINE from those physical objects. Can we ever?

— 0 —

(10)

Ego and Consciousness
(Methodological and Spontaneous acts)

Both consciousness and ego work for us. One works for protection of our life while the other is for protection of our psychic integrity. Ego is more for safeguard of personality meaning our psychological existence in the world.

Consciousness is for saving for life. Whatever physical in us in the body be it the cells, atoms molecules consciousness exerts a protective force for the longest lifetime and is particularly aware whenever danger to life strikes. It alerts you with the sense of pain primarily in case in case some disorders strikes in any of our organ. For ego same sense of protection prevails but it is more concerned with psychic protection. It protects us form mental challenges particularly so when there is danger to disintegration to our personality.

All actions arising from ego activity are methodological and actions springing from consciousness are spontaneous

Ego exists as false boundary at the objective pole of consciousness. It creates psychic objects, in the form of friends, relatives and possessions. It separates what is painful or pleasurable in life and creates conditioned desires for pleasures throughout one's life. It creates a sense of selfhood as "I" for its representation of into the world. This is the name, status, degree, dignity etc. by which we make ourselves known to the world even after our physical demise. Our name and status are our core identity for civic and legal procedures in the society. We continuously gather information about ourselves and about world by taking feedback from others and we put this information as knowledge in our personal gazette. We create an image of ourselves as well as those near to us which is usually not compatible with the reality. This image along with notions becomes faiths and beliefs in the long run and we may be falsely carrying them to the world if we do not continue revising them as the time changes.

All conscious activities must arise from consciousness. In all our transactions, in all the day to day activities consciousness helps to protect our being from all dangers of natural or unnatural occurrence. This becomes particularly clear when we work with fire or electricity or with dangerous animals.

Any action that we perform in the world may be sourced to coming from consciousness or from ego. There is a way to distinguish an action whether it emerges from our ego or our consciousness! We may differentiate ego from consciousness simply from their activities.

Actions arising from ego activity are methodological. They are thought, chosen, worked out and looked for expected results. Consciousness is simply the state of awareness and help to carry out these actions with prime responsibility of protecting life of individual. But sometimes consciousness itself gives origin to certain actions. These actions springing from consciousness are spontaneous. For example when we are deeply affected by humility or attitude of a person, love is a spontaneous feeling which arises from consciousness. When we act with this feeling in mind we act from consciousness.

Spontaneous activity is never thought out first and executed later. Ego activity is procedural, well thought out, scripted in the mind first, weighing all pros and cons and done primarily for promotion or saving of our psychic integrity. Similarly the writing which skims as ego activity is schematic and that from consciousness is spontaneous as seen in creative writing as in poetry. In a letter to someone we are in love we express and pour our heart but in a business letter it is all methodical ego activity. All the prejudices and prejudgments about persons we deal with emerge from ego.

Now the question arises who directs the action. Who at the first place choose a particular action? I may not be wrong if I say that all our worldly actions are chosen by ego. Consciousness telling our body to behave in a way only helps to bring an action to its completion. Here consciousness acts as a slave to our grand ego. But not all our activities are directed by ego. For example when we dance or we sing or we create painting or poetry we are one with the consciousness and these creative acts are so spontaneous that one sees no distinction between inner and outer conscious activity.

Similarly the feelings of selfless love and emotions do appear as activity of consciousness. Emotions are the way by which consciousness relates with the outer. And love being most wonderful out of all emotions. Emotion of love is only exposed to outside when ego is away. Height of conscious activity is one in which all the boundaries of self and world gets dissolved. When we dance on the floor, consciousness becomes one with the action. There occurs spontaneous flow of activity one after the other in form of the movements of dance.

Actions of human are not a small matter; all our actions have cosmic significance. Any action you do goes in the air. It leaves the doer and enters in the world where it gets evaluation and reactions. It reaches to other doers who contribute with their reactions and improvements. The reactions from the world side may again be spontaneous or instantaneous but action may continue visiting the world from one to next doer till an exact reaction from a suitable subject comes back to the original doer when he has all forgotten. It may create turmoil in the life or original doer. When it revisits after such a long interval that person calls it as an act of destiny. One will see it as one's luck, good or bad but will never know it was consequence of one's own action.

In spirituality thought out planned egoistic activities of humans are decried while spontaneous flow of action is encouraged. Persons adopt renunciation (*Sanyaas*) as a way to save them from the bondage or consequences of their actions and create a loving and mindful life so as to return to eternal fold without any unfinished or incomplete action.

All this I am writing during period of history (2012-14) [27]when India is witnessing her own renaissance in the form of protestations against corruption in public life by protesters like Anna Hazare, Arvind Kezriwal & certain others. Should their action be termed as arising from their ego or from consciousness? The way this all appears as well planned, procedural, thought out action and may be said for promotion of their worldly personality, we can say this is an ego activity. But . . . . a big BUT.

All actions have positive or negative consequences. All egoistic actions may give momentary gain to ego but ultimately lead to bondage. But Holy Gita is quite clear on this aspect that actions done for common cause of society do not lead to bondage. So they can never be termed egoistic. But . . . but thinking again as we are not living in times of Gita or Mahabharta. We have collected so much knowledge about ourselves that our ego can deceive others and our own consciousness in a way that what we promote as duty of dharma or common cause may be in your own deep recesses, another ego activity.

---

[27] **2012 Indian anti-corruption movement** is a series of demonstrations and protests across India intended to establish strong legislation and enforcement against perceived endemic political corruption. It was a revival of the 2011 Indian corruption movement which had ended on the last day of the winter session of the Rajya Sabha (Upper house of Indian parliament). The movement restarted with an initial mass gathering at Jantar Mantar, New Delhi on 25 March 2012. Source: http://en.wikipedia.org/wiki/2012_Indian_anti-corruption_movement

But actions of humans when done for community, done as social duty, for a social cause will never be termed egoistic. These actions escape egoism. So says Gita, so says Krishna to Arjuna, that action performed out of sense of one's duty or Dharma i.e. towards a social cause, as collective duty with no thought of selfish gain leads to spiritual fulfillment.

— 0 —

(11)

Intuitive Perception
(What is the Idea of an Idea?)

About knowledge this can be summarized at the end that all knowledge is "knowledge of the knowledge". That means if I have knowledge of something, there is parallel awareness in me that I know. I have knowledge of my own knowledge and I know that things are known to me.

I know that I know. Things known to me become my knowledge and during operation of this knowledge I know that for all knowledge which is known to me, it is easy for me to apply the knowledge and get the results.

By Knowing Things from outside I get the technical knowledge of them and learn more and more about them till they fit into my routine life. That is the "External Knowledge", the source of which is the outer.

Things which run inside me, my inner thoughts and my reactions to the outer things, my inner churnings which gives the knowledge of my inner world and they fit into my behavior, and become my "Internal Knowledge".

The information which comes to me via perceptions gets processed with time. This inner churning or inner processing creates ordered information, reasonably compiled and fully typed. This adds up to my own little wisdom. This is the regular collection and application of knowledge with regular compiling and typing I become well versed in matters of my interest. This may bear fruits in the form of advent of new ideas in mind.

In the event of "an idea" comparatively a new one, running inside me which I might have got as an "Insight" from my own inner wisdom as a result of outward information or inner byproduct of processing. What will I do with that idea? Do I simply visualize that idea, appreciate that idea, have the feeling of it or do something else.

Yes that is the question, of course right one when one come across an entirely new thing and has vague idea or not even the idea. Then how one will proceed? Does he capture this idea with another idea to which he is at least certain?

Idea of an idea is something which needs a very serious contemplative turn of mind. Not an easy adventure indeed. So to make the things simple we can proceed with a very familiar idea at least one which we know fully. Then we can understand how mind makes idea of an idea. The idea may be of an inner vision which may be utterly incommunicable. For example I have the idea of "awareness of my consciousness" or "awareness of my awareness".

Would I put this in my known conceptual frames and communicate to others what it is to be having awareness of the awareness. Do I know it as a feeling or a perception or cognition or merely an item of my knowledge?

Consciousness is the "Internal and infinite essence" of the existence. I may have awareness of this consciousness but do need to tell it to others what this awesome fact is about?

But still I make efforts. To precisely 'know' this idea I would put it in "my known frames". These known frames are my concepts. These concepts are handy and always come to me in a flicker. I know these concepts from my previous learning. As these concepts are fully rationalized so I will start putting this idea in these "rationalized frames". This makes my data adequate. I have reasoned out the inner meaning of that new idea, I would say. But was it a feeling, an interpretation or understanding of the idea?

So that is how I make "idea of an idea". Primary idea was my own inner feeling, my vision while secondary idea was my description of it, first to myself and secondly to others. All ideas of an idea become knowledge of some kind. Mind puts all indefinite vague ideas into known concepts and makes half baked immature knowledge of it so why to take this half baked immature knowledge as definite knowledge.

Mind wants to be definite. Mind has to understand itself and also be able to tell others what mind knows. So mind takes all ideas to the thinking apparatus, to the thoughts, want to associate it to knowledge of some kind. Where already learned concepts of things are there. But why take the ideas in known frames? Why not to take this to something called intuitive perception of an idea.

Intuitive perception of an idea does not mean knowing it by the rational knowledge. It is something knowing by feeling or by simply experiencing it. It is something which every creature does i.e. moving in dangerous area with already exhausted senses i.e. it now senses danger by the sixth sense. Mostly this is done to make the creature alert, which is the prime and natural application of an intuitive perception.

But this can also be used to create a sort of wisdom in you called intuitive wisdom. When you start learning about things at the feeling level. You simply postpone your understanding. You just postpone the conclusions. And after that the intuition will get mature and gives you the exact knowledge of idea in worldly terms.

The internal vision is my inner cognition. It is the intuitive perception of the inner but not the rational perception of it. It is incommunicable but it is at least perceptible to me. This is the idea of my "inner vision". This is bestowed by the nature and this is how nature communicates to her own creatures.

Something which cannot be shared the way it was perceived—is the reality. This is the highest metaphor of reality. Nature looks mysterious because it is not known by knowledge. Reality needs realization not mere understanding.

Then why do I feel it necessary to put all such ideas in known frames and have the knowledge of it. My ideas may of "soul", "conscience", "spirit", "God" etc. all are my little concepts. The totality is the reality and it is highest.

This 'knower—known dyad' (state of being two) is one which creates duality. This is the reality of our daily routine life. This is false perception of reality. In the real perception of reality knower is never different from the known field. He becomes one with the whole in the depth of realization. Knower is the 'observer' and what he observes is the 'observed reality' as today's physics says that observer is the observed. They are one. In the depth of meditation knower becomes known. He is the things he is observing.

Scripture gives you concept, knowledge. Duality-non duality are the concept. But in actuality they are not a matter of understanding. They are the matter of realization. *Vidyayaa Amritum Asnute*—knowledge brings deathless state (Skt.). There is little perceptible difference between 'understanding' and 'realization' for common intellect. But while one is knowledge, other is action (*anubhuti*).

Idea may wear old garb or the borrowed garb or knowledge of others. Repeat it time and again through stale worldly representation of knowledge you would even stop getting understanding leave aside realization.

During realization there is the intuitive perception of the idea. It takes time for the intuition to speak to you. It takes some more transparency of your soul to hear the exact words. But idea is not worldly and it comes from inner depth in different tone and tenor.

Perhaps why every one of us is not bestowed with intuitive perception is because we immediately jump to make idea of an idea. Put that ideas of inner vision in the words and language, rationalize and make knowledge. If ever we let it take the second direction, let it work inside, feel it, sense it till it open up, speak to us in a language very different from our rational words.

Perhaps we have so much demonized the mind that we are seeing it as the real culprit for our growth. Mind is not an entity, it is a function. It is a window like window seven, eight etc. which operates your system. Without mind we will never know there is consciousness and without mind also consciousness will never know there is a world.

— 0 —

(12)

Knowledge and Enlightenment
(Do they compliment or oppose each other?)

Spinoza[28] in mid seventeenth century recorded his observations in his grand treatise 'Ethics'. Regarding knowledge he said that it is an idea of an idea. The primary idea is a flash or insight of consciousness but idea of idea is the knowledge of this insight. It is the reflection over the original idea. It is the expression of the insight in the worldly language. We become known to that insight by putting idea to the knowledgeable frame of mind.

For knowing consciousness through knowledge we create another consciousness. It is the consciousness of consciousness.

---

[28] **Benedictus de Spinoza (1632-1677)** Born in Amsterdam, Spinoza spent his life as a lens grinder. His metaphysical masterpiece, *De ethica*, appeared after his death. In order to retain the notion of God as the one true cause without sacrificing the idea of causality as operative in both the mental and the physical spheres, Spinoza abandoned Descartes' two-substance view. For Spinoza, that single substance was God. Source: http://serendip.brynmawr.edu/Mind/17th.html

We are aware of awareness. We are aware that we are aware. This one is reflective conscious activity of the primary consciousness. We know that we know. This is the awareness of the knowledge. We become conscious of our own knowledge only after advent of knowledge in mind. There always exists knowledge of our knowing and we communicate only knowledge of the knowing. After the original idea is suitably placed in mind we come to know of its presence. For that we create another idea. This idea is the concept, worldly wisdom. Consciousness creates a self-conscious activity; has ability to convey knowledge of our knowing to the world.

How then advent of knowledge takes place in the mind. He talks about the knowledge based on our sensory experience. It is knowledge of both state of our body as well as knowledge of external bodies. This is first kind of knowledge. It is more so an information. We create a separate body of knowledge of all the things known to us in the world. We create catalogue of the information or encyclopedia both in mind as well in the academic books.

Next he talks about knowledge based on our reasoning and our understanding. We define the things based on that knowledge. Based on this knowledge, concepts and definitions of physical as well as sublime i.e. God, of spirit, of world etc. are derived. We create a separate body of knowledge for this too. This is knowledge of second kind.

Further he tells us of a third type of knowledge which is sort of 'mental seeing'. It is sort of inner vision. This is not knowledge of finite things in a finite way. He means to say that there exists a continuity of knowing about ourselves in each moment of our life, within our soul, with in our timeless existence.

Advent of this kind of knowledge into the mind is mind to have an insight or enlightenment.

This is the knowledge of the knowledge in a way that knowledge of first two kinds does not escape from its knowing. Here we place our knowing under our own process of knowing. This is not analytical sort of activity. It is entirely non-judgmental, moment to moment, devoid of concepts and reasoning. Once you start being judgmental you step down to the knowledge of first or second category.

This type of knowledge is related with meta-cognition. By cognition you know through perceptions. Meta-cognition is cognition of cognition. It is the knowing as a state or as a process but not as a knowledge as an end statement, a conclusion. But knowing of this kind is a progression happens with endless continuity. It is the process of knowing of your own cognitive process along with knowing of other stuff.

Kant says the same thing about apperception. This apperception has something to do with perception. Apperception is perception of our perceptions. This may be your *sixth sense,* your insight. We do the perceptions to perceive the outer world; by apperception we perceive our own perceptions. Apperception is a process. If you start building memory and thoughts out of it there starts a process of building knowledge of concepts and conclusions. Then there occur categorization of knowledge as it becomes more superficial and perceptible to ordinary minds.

What if you don't build your memory? Your memory is categorization of knowledge. It is needed for operation of the technical mind. It creates in the mind hard rigid roads which you cannot escape. You drive on these highways and subways only. You rarely enter the next unknown areas. This stuff remains beyond your comprehension. Your knowing changes form a process which is fluid to knowledge which is a solid state. Knowledge merely moves into the known conceptual areas i.e. the fluid state of mind loses its flow. The process of apperception retains fluidity and keeps seamless the endless flow of mind. You may go as far as reading your own thoughts, seeing your own inner self, visualizing consciousness at work!

Kant differentiates apperception into two—One is empirical apperception—which is perception of states of body which again is moment to moment. It is of lower kind and attaches you to the body. You develop your tastes or behavior as per your empirical apperception. Second is Transcendental Apperception. "This is pure, original, unchangeable consciousness which is the necessary condition of experience as such and the ultimate foundation of the synthetic unity of experience", says Kant.

This means you observe the self not as in its state of hilarity or sadness, excitement or frustration, hunger or thirst. Once you move inside you observe this stuff first. By doing so you are empirically attached to your self. You'll have to transcend this sort of apperception. When you are not affected by states of self, its happy or sad mood you transcend. You don't care for selfhood even. You reduce yourself to a point, with nothingness all around. You are then but one with all of unity of self with the universe.

That is what to say of reflection. Sartre also differentiates Pure and Impure reflection. In impure reflection, self contemplates upon its psychic states. Pure reflection is the presence of reflective consciousness to the consciousness reflected on. It is the immediate non cognitive consciousness of the self.

If someone asks me, what was I doing just a moment ago? To answer this I do not have to go to my memory. I immediately can answer that. There exists an immediate non cognitive relation of mine with myself. Why non-cognitive because it was not through thought activity. While I was busy with the outer I was not deliberately thinking of myself at the same time. But later on this becomes clear that I had the perception of myself during an intense state of outer activity too.

During an action if you are injured you do not feel pain till the action is over. You feel pain only when you reflect over the body. So action is a forward activity. Memory of action is when you deliberately think over your past acts.

But your memory is not consciousness. It is stored knowledge Memory means positing your past activity, to the stored compartments. Consciousness does not run backward. It is continuous forward process. When consciousness moves in memory stores, this is branching of its forward activity. This is an additional engagement of consciousness, an additional burden.

In over burdened and excessively engaged consciousness, consciousness activity is blunted. Its RAM (Random Access Memory of computer) is occupied. So it creates its hard disc. It enters into the process of creating a body of memory and knowledge, both worldly and personal. It enters into the process of separation and naming entire objective world. These are the Akashic records of consciousness. Consciousness which can never leave past is sluggish with the engagement of the world.

This means for better dealing with other persons we create their past records. This in simple sense is to aid memory. We better remind persons by giving prejudiced account to their personalities and ultimately become victim of a plethora of conditioned responses from this dealing. We fail to understand as we are changing in every moment other people might have changed a lot with time.

To be reflectively consciousness does not mean to be self conscious. Phenomenon of self consciousness does not lead you to any spiritual experience. A child becomes self conscious when a group of elders ask him to recite his latest learned nursery rhyme. He loses confidence and loses more than half of his performance.

We become self conscious while on stage or sometimes alone we are sad or happy or someone has hurt or admired us. During meditation if we are just contemplating over our thoughts activity, seeing only the state of self being affected by thoughts of happiness or sadness we are into state of impure reflection only. For pure reflection to happen, we are to become reflectively conscious!

But this pure reflection to happen it requires a catharsis, purging of the past affected by consciousness on itself. It is akin to scanning and defragmentation of the computer hard disc. Its details are in the next chapter.

— 0 —

(13)

Catharsis

(Cleansing of the Thinking Soul)

Word catharsis is Aristotelian term which means purification or cleansing. This is to cleanse all aspects of our physical existence. We exist at different levels and in many realms. First one, quite perceptible to everyone is the realm of physical or physiological existence. We as a physical body exist in nature i.e. in the universe. Being chemical ourselves we are exposed to physical and chemical forces of nature. We are also exposed to other biological forces in the form of other creatures, like bacteria and viruses. The living organism in us with aid of immunity that builds up with time resists many of these forces. We resist them up till the end of our life. Ultimately these forces as singularly or in multiple win and we are no more in our life. As we eat from nature and put our wastes into it, we are bound to get infested with many harmful forms of life as well as we are bound to get dirty and soiled, get polluted and heavily laden with chemicals we are exposed with.

The things we eat are of two kinds. Things we prefer because of their taste and things we prefer as per their nutritional value. The tastier material becomes our fixation because of the excessive quantity we take or its dubious quality. We burden our systems with overfeeding and at certain stage we need to cleanse our systems by taking healthier food which may not be tastier. As we cleanse our external body by taking bath and clothing ourselves to protect from dusty winds and sun so we cleanse the internal parts by fasting and eating right kind of food.

We exist as mind or ego in our body and primary expression of this is the creation of thoughts. We are what our thoughts are. Our thoughts create a psychic being in us and this being continues to guide our whole life. We create a particular pattern of chemical activity in the brain which is manifested if mild in the form of routine display of emotions and if exaggerate in the form of obsessions and fetishes. Our thoughts take root in the deep emotional state of mind and in turn the thoughts start creating a definite pattern of emotions. Once created this pattern of thought and emotional activity does not leave us for long. They create a model of cyclical activity in us. Circular thoughts do not leave us for fair observation. We simply can't wish them away. These thoughts create parallel emotions which put thought and temperament of mind in a vicious loop. The same emotions and same thoughts are repeated for an unlimited period.

Progenitor of the thoughts is emotions of certain kind. So before dealing with thought activity we have to deal with the emotions. We have to deal with type of being we have made of our self. Since our childhood we have been dealing with the emotional activity in us. We cannot recollect a single incidence when we have not reacted to our friends or parents without emotions.

For cleansing our thoughts we must give attention to this emotional realm. We are over laden with different types of emotions at all periods of time e.g. waking, sleeping, and dreaming and childhood, adult and old age. We attach these emotions unnecessarily with our thoughts and end up with conditioning of our emotions and thoughts. We call them as emotional thoughts but these two are actually a dual pair. With a particular emotion arising comes automatically a particular thought activity which does not allow the emotion to die away.

As said earlier these emotions are chemical activity occurring in our brain and hormonal glands. It comes and goes and does not stay longer. For example a powerful emotion like fear reverberates in all our systems and puts us upside down. But fear state does not stay longer. When the chemical activity subside fear also goes away. But we unnecessary attach fear with our memory & thoughts which keeps alive the situation, time etc. and fear keeps on revisiting us whenever the same situation strikes. We remember the past and cannot comprehend the novelty of next situation which may not be that much fearful. So it becomes necessary to cleanse ourselves of all similar emotions from our body before moving further in our expedition in spiritual field.

But ultimately our existence is in totality and not fractionalized. We need a thorough cleansing of our existence if we want to move to subtler realms. We need not only individual emotional, mental or psychic cleansing but also collective social cleansing. A person who has individually cleansed himself will interact with the society which is not similarly cleansed. So his next step is to invoke similar cleansing activity in society. Perhaps that was why the great spiritual persons in history like Buddha or Christ took the task of social cleansing to divest people of their unclean thoughts.

More such realms can be mental or psychic, intellectual, moral, religious and spiritual and many similar subtle realms we might still not know. For example the intellectual cleansing asks us to relearn our experiences for which we have assigned erroneous academic terms. Every new entrant in the field of intellectuality does the same job. Most of our spiritual & religious teachers come in this category too. Academic terminology in spirituality only enhances our intellectual learning but does not contribute to the realization of reality in totality. The total realization experience which may be called spiritual experience comes only when we move above the understanding.

To separate our "total existential experience" into kinds of realms—physical and physiological, emotional, intellectual, religious and or spiritual—is to show how we can apply principles of catharsis to cleanse these different levels of existence.

To cleanse the interiority and exteriority of our existence we should always start from the exterior. Correct eating and cleaning habits must be properly and disciplinarily observed. We must give attention to the areas where we join interior with the exterior. How the exterior deviation in the habits create our interior compulsions. How a particular food become our fetish. How over cleansing and exterior decoration of the body create similar perfectionist attitude in our mind and lead to obsession and fixation with cleanliness. Reading our aesthetic—hedonic areas of mind, we encounter our physical drives and bodily pleasures. The need for catharsis in this primary area is not a one time job. It is frequently done than in any other realm. For that we simply keep away from the hedonistic areas of world and mind both. All our dietary and sexual pleasures put body & mind in conditioned mode and are obstacles for the spiritual experience.

Here, catharsis consists of withdrawing oneself from all external attractions and if one can't move to serene neutral environment then it is done by restraining and channelizing our internal longings. It is not essential that we should altogether shun world of desire and adopt an ascetic life. We rather should stop ourselves encouraging and nourishing our primordial drives. We channelize them by moving to more creative fields.

What separates man from the beasts is whether he controls his drives or whether they control him. Any unrestrained activity by man can be brutish, be it unrestrained sex or violence or unrestrained desire for higher worldly status. Any uninhibited display of sexual passions can be brutish and dehumanizing. Man succumbs to a frenzy of primitive passions and start treating his partners as things, which means he is centered to fulfill his desire only. However within a framework sexual experience becomes something beautiful and sacred. It is always not that you engage with your partner in physical sexual mode. You can mentally enjoy her/ his presence in close and distant proximity. Later on you may derive spiritual experience from sexual union of two souls. Furthermore, it actually becomes a vehicle for certain natural outcome such as procreation i.e. of progeny as well as procreation of creative energy in you.

Man's natural biological drives are not altogether wrong. These in themselves are necessary for survival, and can become good or evil when performed ruthlessly. At worst, in a relentless quest for gratification of his ever-increasing desires, man can become criminal and depraved, almost satanic. On the other hand, if one exercises control over these natural urges and channelize them for worldly & non-worldly pursuits they can be a force for good.

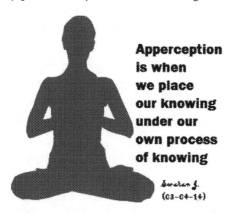

Apperception is when we place our knowing under our own process of knowing

Swaran J.
(03-04-14)

Catharsis is purification and cleansing process of these prime desires of body and mind. As we restrict our physical movements to an area of pleasure & temptations we equally restrict our thoughts and emotions to prevent their attachment to them. To altogether stop our emotional clinging to a particular thought we may create a frustrated being in us. This emotional frustration will create a form of apathy and may take us to self deterioration and emotional detachment from the world. We need not to do this so emotions are not frustrated but are sufficiently rinsed out, sufficiently lived out so that they do not further affect our thought in any way. To start with emotions are understood but not acted out. Next they are simply felt at deep mental level. Then emotions are experienced in their purity without any attachment to thoughts or to the events of our life. Later our emotional mental field becomes so much regulated and in our control that acting upon an emotion does not develop into an impulsive act. We do not create a reactionary mind or animal mind to emotions.

This of course does not mean that we'll have to blunt our emotions. We are not to become an emotionally dead. Like an animal. Emotional catharsis actually means to be able to control blast of emotions. As in psychology we create abreaction or relive an emotional experience in order to reduce or abolish emotional trauma. The live experience is created in controlled environment as to release the lethal effects of traumatic experience in the past.

We do not control emotions or put lid over them. We do not intellectually understand them to stop them there & then. We even do not divide emotions into good and bad and those which are easy to express and others not so. But ultimate practice is to live out emotions so that they do not interfere in reasoning and realizing reality. They do not interfere with your sound reactions to the other players.

Every emotion creates around it an emotional field. It is linked to a large number of ideas. Love for a person brings to the mind many pictures and words about him. Similarly, anger produces many pictures and words in the mind. By themselves, images and words are harmless. It is the impulses and conditioned reactions connected to them that create all the trouble.

Once we have dealt with our emotions then dealing with our thoughts become easier. We must understand that before every thought there was a thoughtless state of the mind e.g. when you have just risen from bed unless you are not preoccupied with previous day hectic schedule. You might have enjoyed this thoughtless state in your deep sleep. Sleep should be dreamless or at least most of its part. Dreams are actually our thoughts in image form. Excessive and forgetful dreaming only shows excess thought activity.

Thoughts like emotions are also lived out. Your thoughts are your life issues which you have not dealt with properly. You can deal with the current issues so that they do not become senseless thoughts after time has passed. Older issues which you cannot deal now become a futile thought activity. These are the thoughts which must be cleansed from the mind's disc. They are dispassionately watched. You watch your own thought activity as a second observer. You put mind's disc in scanner mode. You simply see them come and go. You do not interfere with then. Even the most brutal thought which has the capacity to hurt you mentally is dealt in the same way. You must be able to stay on such thoughts as computer deals with some odd file. You do not let such thought pass out or branch to other petty thought. Now you can intellectually deal with it or like emotions live it out. It might remind you time and again of your failures. Time and again you watch such thoughts you start living them and then creating a dispassionate attitude for them. Ultimately they die away. This is in one way to complete the thought process for one particular thought or issue so as to close it forever. So that it does not raise its head in one's thoughts. If we know the reason and effect of one particular thought then we are able to handle it intelligently.

All our art and literature is an act to relive and exterminate our thoughts. Rather all art, poetry, paintings, drama and other forms of literature help us to affect this emotional and thought catharsis. While reading literature, an epic or a novel or by visualizing drama we identify ourselves with the characters and try to relive the situations which may have happened in our lives in similar or different ways. This too causes a cathartic effect on our emotions.

Actually thoughtless mind is not devoid of thoughts. Creative thoughts will never disappear from the mind. Thoughtless mind is the linear mind. It creates linear, forward and non-repetitive thoughts. It does not indulge in useless circular thought activity where same thought is repeated thousand times in a single day. It creates superior thoughts which help to understand life better. A single insightful thought clears away all our doubts and ignorance. It is prophetic and gives us inner vision. But such insightful thoughts are blocked by the futile thought activity or reckless worldly pursuits. We must do them way, take a serene position both physically and mentally to experience higher state of mind with visionary thoughts.

There is one Christian idea of Kenosis in which one does 'Self-emptying' of all his personal wills and desires in order to become 'entirely receptive to divine will'. This is to make oneself 'the vessel' of God's desires and attributes. Hindu philosophy moves further with the idea of *samskaras*. *Samaskaras* are the latent impressions within the mind. They give rise to desires, emotional impulses, instinctual drives etc. and also included are those which give rise to concepts, ideas to our normal thinking. We are particularly attached to certain ideas and concepts which impart us a particular religious or philosophical position. All this is because of the *samaskaras* of the family one is born into. Hindu philosophy believes them to be impressions of one's past lives. But rationally we can understand them as mind molding from the early childhood. We cannot budge away from those impressions. To deal with life correctly and open heartedly we must also get rid of them.

Emotions create their own control at the times of reliving staged emotions. We feel easy to experience our emotions at the time of seeing other people emoting. That was how the idea of drama started in almost all ancient human civilizations. We know not only great Greek tragedies, and comedies as well but also great dramatists like Kalidasa, Bhasa on Indian ground. Here we can deduct why so these dramas, staged as well as done in movies and TV soap operas have occupied so much mental space of our today's life.

Not only drama all our literature, art paintings etc caters to our innate needs of emotional catharsis. A visitor to the French impressionist painter Matisse pointed to some nudes hanging on the wall and asked him:

"Don't you think these have a demoralizing effect on people?"

The artist calmly replied,

"My dear man, it is not a woman, it is only a picture. An artist sees only a picture in a woman, whereas an ordinary man sees a woman in a picture—this is the difference between the two." This does not of course mean that all artists are holy sages. But in them the creative urge becomes so strong that it produces a certain degree of detachment— aesthetic detachment as it is called.

So as to cause catharsis we create a sort of emotional detachment in all our transactions. As this is not easy and feasible for everyone great Yogi's, Indian spiritual mystics have created disciplinary methodology for this. One method is to weaken the power of the impulses through abstinence, avoidance, withdrawal and other forms of *tapas* or austerity. Another method is to increase the number of good *samskaras* through virtuous *karma*.

Patanjali[29], great Yogi of Indian Yoga system speaks of a third method, which may be practiced long with the other two.

This is to change the connection between impulses and mental images. This process of changing the connections between mental images and impulses is called *pratipaksa-bhavanam*. This is to be done through proper self-analysis, but this becomes effective only when the new connections are tested in action. A yet higher state is to detach the will. The connection between images and impulses is consciously made by exercising the will. To detach this will from the impulses is not an easy task.

For detailed study one may refer to "Raja Yoga—Yoga Aphorisms of Patanjali" by Swami Vivekananda.

But still, it is not the goal—because what will happen to all your impressions that you have gathered in the past?

---

[29]   **Patanjali*:** Undoubtedly the greatest expounder of Yoga, lived sometime between 500 and 200 B.C. The life of Patanjali is an enigma to modern historians, and almost nothing is known about this great Master who epitomizes Yoga. Source: http://www.iyengaryoga.in/life_patanjali.htm

Many, many lives your forefathers have lived, acted, reacted and passed on their impressions to you. You have done many things, undone many things. What will happen to it? Conscious mind has become pure; conscious mind has dropped even the activity of purity. But the unconscious is vast and there you carry all the seeds, the blueprints. They are within you.

Indian system of Yoga relies on the activation or revisiting of seven chakras or energy centers. These are the anatomical and physiological levels of spinal cord and associated sympathetic and parasympathetic trunks (great nerves) in us. These levels cater to smooth functioning different body parts like digestive, urinary and reproductive system, moving on to lungs and heart and then speech centers in throat and brain reaching via frontal lobe up to the crown of skull and brain. These internal parts represent the internal unconscious functions of the body. Though being unconscious still they respond to internal will of body. Body's will is different from the external will. Basically one cannot willfully modify the functions of body or his thought activity. Yoga system of revising these centers will align the body's will to the one's own will.

These centers start from *Muladhara* Chakra i.e. spinal center at the base of spine near the Rectum or anal canal. This spinal center remains dormant and inactivated during most part of our early life and creates hurdles in our long personal journey towards enlightenment. These are knots, which act as barriers to the free flow of *prana* or energy in lowest centers. The energy which should flow back through spinal cord upward during meditation as you are now revisiting each energy center or chakra. When first level is reactivated we remove the biggest hurdle. We have just made conscious the unconscious energy flow in us. Yogis say that this unconscious energy or '*prana*' is lying coiled at this level. Making it conscious is an uncoiling activity which directs the energy flow towards brain.

When we stop at the second the *Swadhisthana* chakra, we just win our hypersexual activity, and become celibate. When we stop at third the *Manipura* chakra we win our hunger and desires of food. At *Anaahat* chakra the next we win the emotional being in us and become strong in terms emotions and heart. When stop at *Vishudha* chakra we win our '*vani*', the voice or the speech and discourse and are able to lecture or speak endlessly, reasonably and rhythmically. When stop at next '*Agya* chakra' we win our intellectuality and grow our personality. But only real *jnana* (knowledge) opens in us when we reach final *Sahsarara* chakra. This culminates in the final state of enlightenment where the person not only knows his being but also the relation of this being to the universe.

To enter into this supreme meditative state Patanjali divides the unconscious into two. To delve into the unconscious we enter into the Samadhi or meditative state. He speaks of *Sabeej* Samadhi—when the unconscious is there and mind that is the will with which you have stared meditation has been dropped consciously, it is a Samadhi with seeds—*Sabeej*. When those seeds are also burned, then you attain the perfect—the *Nirbeej* samadhi: samadhi without seeds. You enter into the depth of unconscious which is real you. The external you as will, desire, or executive is not here.

But this is the first step; many are misguided—they think this is the last because it is so pure and you feel so blissful and so happy that you think that now nothing is there to be achieved more. If you ask Patanjali, he will say this is just the first *Samadhi*. It is not the final, the ultimate; ultimate is still far away.

A man of positive reasoning will discard all thoughts that are not his own. They are not authentic; he has not found them through his own experience. He has accumulated from others, borrowed. They are dirty. Then you can create your own thoughts. And a thought that is created by you is really potential: it has a power of its own. But thought may be of others or one's own all cater to mental activity in us. So he talks of *Asamprajanata* Samadhi. In Asamprajnata Samadhi, there is a cessation of all mental activity, and the mind only retains unmanifested impressions. First type of Samadhi is attainment of purity of unconscious; second is disappearance of this purity even because even the purest is impure because it is there. First there was "I" present during Samadhi later on just "amness" was there. Now both I and amness must go. Disappearance of the purity also, is *asamprajnata*. There is a cessation of all mental activity you have cut down the tree completely. You have burned the seeds too.

— 0 —

(14)

End of Desire
(I Hug the Me within Me)

All desires are desires to reach the object of the desire

Object of the desire is forever away

Always illusory it remains

Desire of desire is never reached

Thought tries hard again and again

Object of the desire is beyond the flesh

The flesh is mere the iceberg tip

The flesh is mere the comely grip

Desire for flesh is not desire of layer

Beyond the flesh is someone there

Beyond the flesh is next me

Beyond the flesh is next reality

Me that flies to reach object of desire

Is the me that flies to the next me

The me that flies to reach next me

Is the me who wants to escape from me

The me who tries to escape from me

Is the me that lives in the dark

The me that lives in the dark

This me tries hard to be naked stark

This me always horrifies me

This me always mortifies me

to escape from that I create desires

This me needs my healing hug

This me is the end of all my desires.

Me within Me

That me that needs my healing hug
This me is the end of all my desires
Swaran J. (04-04-14)

— 0 —

(15)

Thoughts and Transparent Mind
(Thinking the Thoughtless)

What we often express when we talk to others? Why are we ever compulsive to converse with others. Why is there a deep inner urge to communicate? Why do we communicate actually? Why do we put ourselves in dialogue with others?

The act of communication per se is a means to coordinate our thoughts with thoughts of others and less as mere expresssions of our feelings. We are unique & individual beings but we perceive this uniqueness as an odd quality. Sometimes we are so overwhelmed with our individuality that we find ourselves too strange and solitary and we communicate to find whether others are like us too! We communicate to share this uniqueness. We communicate to get ourselves generalized. In any way we are not compatible with our uniqueness.

When we communicate we find an extraordinary change in ourselves. We are affected by the thoughts of others. The level at which we think alike gives us respite. By arguments and raising counterpoints we reach at some reasonable position.

We are affected by our own thoughts. The inner environment of our psyche is never in peace. We are continously engaged with our thoughts while dealing with the world. But are we alone subjected to such kind of activity of thoughts. Why at first palce have we thoughts?

When we are concerned with whys and hows of the matter, we see that our subjective feelings are generally in clash with the objectified world. We want to convey our feelings to the world, to our fellows. Our fellows may be having entirely different feelings and different thoughts.

If ever we just change the subjective position with our fellows. Like we change our seat in a bus or train. We put ourselves in their head and hearts and read their thought and actions. Like a writer we may understand his inner feelings.

For this we will have to have a transparent mind. Like an author who has a tansparent mind. He can project his subjectivety in any on member of *Homo sapiens* and even in inanimate objects and other primordial forms of life. He can understands that his inner reactions are just representative reactions of the others. Perhaps that is why a writer can write about the innermost feelings of a saint and a tyrant with equal ease. But is it the prerogative of writers and artists only, as distinct from others to act with such empathy?

To say the least it is that of a transparent mind. Can't we create such a transparent mind in ourselves. A mind which can watch itself even while engaged with the outer world; a mind that do not interfere by its biases and prejudgements while forming the reactions; a mind that can act like a mirror which reflects everything and take nothing; a mind which is a pure energy or a mind which is not a mind at all.

Such an open mind while treading the thorny path of life collects many gems of eternal truth. What if this never fading truth is reproduced in the form of poetry, stage or cinema or communiques and blogs on the web pages. Though they make the feelings generalized but contribute to some sort of general understanding.

However there is a confused arena of thoughts too. People with their egoistic tendencies and utter untruthfullness to their own feelings have created chaos and disorder. They do not convey what they actually feel. They show to the world their generalized side only. A young enterant in the world experience bewilderment when he sees is a wide chiasm between what the people feel and what they express. There is wide gap between the two. This external chaos what this gap creates compounds his internal confusion.

But a transparent mind sets the record straight. He questions and struggles to find answers. He expresses what is generally considered inexpressible. His thought though works in a limited field but has an ability to clarify the things in a certain way. Such a thought illuminate all other thoughts. Such thoughts from transparent mind are complete thoughts.

This is a pure thought which pierces the mind like a sword and can move without any undue exercise of control on the part of the receipient. Such pure thought cleanses the mind of all troublesome and worrisome thoughts. It is a way of catharsis in which thoughts end by ending themselves. This will eventually lead to the blessed state of thoughtlessness.

Why aren't we always blessed with such pure thoughts? Why we are continuously visited upon by old, stale thoughts? Despite all distress and agony that we experience from this activity why don't we get liberated from this at all? We are we always in the habit of thinking in a limited field on the same lines and pattern.

A thought creates an affect which is necessary for its own survival. It gives the mind the luxury of riding on its back and experience that affect. The mind jumps like a grasshopper from one thing to another. Till mind remains attached to this ordinarily pleasurable activity, it stretches it to any length.

But with exercise of little awareness one starts observing the futility of this restless act. The gradual strengthening of this awareness, which we now term as the observer in us stifles the unrestrained freedom of thoughts. But this is very unlikely to occur if this observer is under the intellectual spell.

Due to this the observer adopts the path of rationality. It would give many explanations and justifications to our various acts and motives in the world. It keeps on moving with its curious and curious theorizations till is lost in the endless world of cause and effect. Ultimately it will create its own prison in the form of fixed ideology which takes it farther and farther away from the reality.

The real observation is rather non-reactional attentiveness. Can you observe your thoughts without analysing them; without giving them any justification; without entertaining their affect? You simply attend them without becoming elated or morbid.

This happens only when you simply watch your weakness and donot comment upon this as your own weakness but term it as weakness of the mankind; when good and bad for you are just two parts of the whole; when you discover for yourself there exists in the world an absolute goodness and relative goodness and discover further that relative goodness is as bad as bad because it is always raised against bad; when you strive for higher goodness which donot rely upon the bad for its survival. It does not disapproves the bad; with such an attitude you've freed yourself from the world of opposites.

Then you've freed yourself from that agonising activity of thoughts produced by undue reactions within your mind. When there is little thought activity within the mind there is enough free space to confront ever changing life; enough time to concentrate upon other creative activities of the mind and there is release of immence energy.

— 0 —

(16)

Immortality or Biological Survival
(We have both!)

Human race is immortal and so is all the biological life on earth. We've survived biologically is evident from the fact that human race is now more than two million years old and we are roughly seven billion bodies on earth.

If we believe evolutionary ladder next should some higher species replace this man and what we should call it. For better word which will be coined in future we may call that man the "Higher man" or "Super-man". The evolution of higher man whenever it happens will put present man in the similar situation in which now is the monkey? Animals-Monkey-Man triad in the past will be replaced as Animals-Man-Higher man in the future. What will be the status of present man then, rues Nietzsche in one of his major writing.

That means present man will be like a human monkey or human ape to the higher man. Concurrent evolution of human consciousness is quite necessary to put whole of present human race in the next series of evolution. This can only be accomplished if we collectively as a race get harmonized to physical & psychological ways of living, adopt collective thinking and shed away the individualized values; and if all humans on this earth could create oneness at the level of thought.

This thinking is basic to the philosophy of Nietzsche, the philosopher. He once announced to the world that God is dead. We find scores of interpreters reminding us here and there on different web pages calling him a mere mortal and rather a fool who himself is no more. Should now the God, omnipotent one, announce his death to the publishers who published his words, contend some of them. There may be some reason in this contention.

But examining critically and moving to another dimension we find a big fallacy here. Whenever someone refers to Nietzsche, regarding some significant point he emphasized in his books, reader with simple curiosity will go to the book to read it. Now reader cannot deny the fact that Nietzsche is there in his words! Speaking in first person!! You may despise him or you may admire him, but Nietzsche is there in his books.

And now suddenly strikes the idea of creator and creation in the readers mind. He finds Nietzsche right there in his creations as God is believed to be, in the nature or universe—His creation. He finds Nietzsche speaking his words and he attends him while he reads his words.

You may still be hesitant to accept this idea of immortality. But won't you agree that conventional model of immortality cannot be decided on the grounds where on one side you have an 'imagined' and archetypal God while on other an ordinary mortal as Nietzsche, who once created extraordinary works.

In that way, you startle to find, this sort of immortality can be assigned to any philosopher, painter or poet or similar creator. Yes—why not! But what about those ordinary mortals who were not fortunate enough to do some everlasting work of fame during their life time? Why they are not immortal?

Yes, they also live in their creations viz. house they built or the trees they planted. They also live in the memory of their friends, well-wishers and relatives. But all these are perishable things including memory, you argue. Where is now placed our newly invented immortality formula?

A plant or an animal or human produce replica of themselves as offspring and tend to live after the original form dies or parishes. We can say that we are here on this earth because of the genetic material supplied by our fore-fathers. Actually we are they and they are living through us. This is the biological chain of survival which has not perished since millions of years.

The relationship of nature with the species from its very inception was harsh enough to force the species to choose this mode of survival. This biological survival does not pertain merely to survival of individual genetic material of a single member of the species but rather to all the members or whole genre or whole evolutionary chain. If one member dies without producing offspring whole of the species does not go extinct.

But failure of this biological survival is also be there in evolutionary history. Immortality won't exist when one particular species entirely goes extinct, just like Dinosaurs etc. Quite reasonable doubt!

This word extinction as applied to Dinos may not be correct. Species might have moved to co-lateral evolutionary chains before going extinct and it may be still surviving! For example Dinosaurs evolved as birds.

Therefore one may live in many subsequent generations in one or other way. All of the creatures on this earth, unspecified, all the mortal ones, form an unbroken immortal chain of life. These varied species are tactics of nature's diversity plans and life in us is the final core of unity.

The logic may sound good but pertains to physical side of the evolution. All the amoeba, bacteria, viruses and higher forms of life, as one life are all surviving. But our original idea, the survival within consciousness of the life forms—is still unexplored.

Besides our physical evolution there occurs concurrent evolution of consciousness which is guided by society's major philosophical and cultural factors.

So the evolution of consciousness in the species may not always go in such survival mode. Nietzsche' work may not survive the test of time, may be destroyed by the book-worms or by some prejudiced rulings in an fanatical state may be may be consigned to flames and this may happen to any other similar works of varied authors which are disliked and destroyed. Or we can say all such works of previous centuries will eventually be passed into oblivion and forgotten by materially passionate future generations. Or you can irrationally think that once you've stopped teaching a work in the academic circles or removed from the shelves the author will be eventually forgotten. Where would you find Nietzsche with his ilk surviving then?

No, that is not! Think again!

You can physically destroy the work of an author you don't like. But can you straighten the bend that Nietzsche was able to produce in the mind and consciousness of contemporary and forthcoming generations. This bend may be of Darwin or Newton or Einstein or Nietzsche or any such author. Can you erase the societal changes from the consciousness of then and future societies?

All this has strong scientific basis. Basic unit of evolution in our biological life is 'gene' while unit of evolution in consciousness is 'meme'. Meme[30] is a unit of human cultural transmission. As you understand that genes undergo evolutionary changes the memes too undergo evolutions. Rather there is meme & gene co-evolution.

---

[30] **Meme:** The word *meme* is a shortening (modeled on *gene*) of *mimeme* (from Ancient Greek) meaning "to imitate", and it was coined by the British evolutionary biologist Richard Dawkins in The Selfish Gene as a concept for discussion of evolutionary principles in explaining the spread of ideas and cultural phenomena. Examples of memes given in the book included melodies, catch-phrases, fashion, and the technology of building arches. Source: http://en.wikipedia.org/wiki/Meme

A meme is a recognized scientific term which means an idea or a speck of behavior which spreads from person to person within a culture. Meme is new fad for scientists ever since Richard Dawkins wrote the book 'The Selfish Gene'[31] published in 1976.

A meme acts as a unit for carrying cultural ideas, symbols or practices, which can be transmitted from one mind to another through writing, speech, gestures, rituals or other imitable phenomena.—said meme scientist Graham[32] in 2002.

Supporters of the concept regard memes as cultural analogues to genes and like genes they self-replicate, mutate and respond to selective pressures. Proponents theorize that memes may evolve by natural selection in a manner analogous to that of biological evolution.

Memes do this through the processes of variation mutation, competition and inheritance, each of which influences a

---

[31] **Clinton Richard Dawkins (born 1941)** is an English evolutionary biologist and writer. *The Selfish Gene* is a book on evolution published in 1976. Dawkins used the term "selfish gene" as a way of expressing the gene centered view of evolution as opposed to the views focused on the organism and the group, The book also coins the term meme for a unit of human cultural evolution analogous to the gene, suggesting that such "selfish" replication may also model human culture, in a different sense. Memetics since then has become the subject of many studies since the publication of the book. Source: http://en.wikipedia.org/wiki/Meme

[32] **Graham, Gordon (2002),** *Genes: a philosophical inquiry*, New York: Routledge, p. 196, ISBN 0-415-25257-1
Source: http://en.wikipedia.org/wiki/Meme

meme's reproductive success. Memes spread through the behaviors that they generate in their hosts. Memes that propagate less prolifically may become extinct, while others may survive, spread and mutate. Memes that replicate most effectively enjoy more success, and some may replicate effectively even when they prove to be detrimental to the welfare of their hosts wrote Kelly et al[33] in1994.

Basic unit of evolution in our biological life is 'gene' 'Meme' is a unit of human cultural transmission

Swaran J. (28-03-14)

Thus we do survive in others even after our demise with our views and behavior. With strong views and strong behavior the chances of survival is even more.

As some exemplary figure survives in us as a particular mind like Gandhi in Gandhians, Marx in Marxists the less perfect & naïve one does survive too as a collective psyche. These are not only forms of mind but also survival of a personality in us which is held in esteem may be locally or globally.

---

[33] **Kelly, Kevin (1994)**, *Out of control: the new biology of machines, social systems and the economic world*, Boston: Addison-Wesley, p. 360, ISBN 0-201-48340-8 Source: http://en.wikipedia.org/wiki/Meme

This type of mind does not die easily. To create such type of exemplary immortality one needs extraordinary conditions of mind, body and coexisting circumstances.

What Nietzsche meant when he said, 'God is dead' was about the psychological God which was able to survive in the mind of millions of generations till reasoning and enlightenment dawned upon man. This enlightenment actually gave birth of altogether new man who vehemently wiped off the ritualistic man which tradition has put in his body and psyche. Enlightened man is going to exist in many future generations and one day he may get further overridden by next new man.

— 0 —

(17)

Evolutionary Mutation
(Some contradictory aspects)

Evolutionary mutation in the human consciousness vis-a-vis in human physico-genetic makeup is as much a matter of debate as it may be of delightful veneration. The learned consciousness groups, the gurus, the saints, the bloggers, the seekers of highest wisdom continuously talk about it.

Most conscientious among men, for example Christ was talking about it right since dawn of civilization calling it entering into "God's Kingdom" thereby differentiating it from the man's own self managed kingdom on the earth. This God' kingdom is again worldly because manifest part of all that is hidden is carried out before our physical eyes.

These days scientists contend, in fact methodically, how a critical mass of *Homo sapiens* if take initiative to change will evolve forever. This critical mass is achieved when a sufficient number out of whole race of humanity change or evolve by achieving the higher sort of physical and mental behavior.

They may adopt (perhaps!) some childlike innocence, leave aside the world of rulers and ruled, adopt a new way of collective oneness and start living without any trace of personalized ego and present day management. After creating that sufficient critical number out of whole population of earth humanity will be prepared to take that collective shift in their consciousness and man will be ready for the next evolutionary mutation. Others who fail for the first time will follow the suit more easily as one swimmer will assist in the swimming of many or simple inspirational process will do the job. All speculations end with a big perhaps!

These consciousness groups take efforts to inform their audience about the consequences of such mutation and they are willingly or unwillingly accepting that world will no longer be pure black or white, pure good or pure bad because all these ideas of good and bad are the derivatives of our personalized ego.

There will be many shades of gray and all the things with good and bad tags will again be there not as our primitive tribal hostility towards the unfamiliar but as an acceptance for the diverse. The love we talk of everyday will become the real affection for the fellow and underprivileged creation. Perhaps . . . so happens. Can't say!

Shall we be able to discontinue all efforts of making this earth and this whole universe our own personal enterprise by then? The earth and this universe belong to its inhabitants, animal or men and we must submit to highest will of creation and destruction to the biological elements in us. Shall we voluntarily abdicate all our rights to rule over whole minor and major forms of creation? Not sure.

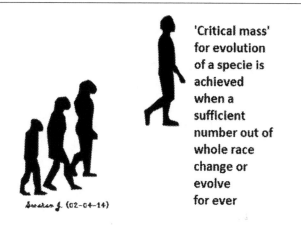

'Critical mass'
for evolution
of a specie is
achieved
when a
sufficient
number out of
whole race
change or
evolve
for ever

Swaran J. (02-04-14)

This may be added here that good and bad in today's world are relative and often unmerciful towards each other. Good becomes as bad as bad when it is raised against the bad. The good we create in the form of morals monitoring behavior of our fellow kin much less our own.

While we ourselves indulge in certain infallibilities but we don't let others to do so without falling prey to criticism. The ethical guards of the society along with their rebels, heroes and anti heroes demonstrate their personal ideas of good and bad so practically that they never give the damn to the public loss of life and property. This collectively is termed as collateral damage!

The consciousness groups collectively call for an end to such battles of demonic gods and godly demons and constantly remind men to re-assign nature to take the roles to rear or raze our existence.

It may be however added that end of good and bad as relative forces must not become the end of absolute goodness which must always be there as a guiding principle to our existence and which is always be different from our personal ideas about good and bad. Similarly absolute evil is not evil but a tool in the hands of the nature's to destroy and create new. Meaning thereby when a terrorist strikes a busy block it is nature's hidden plan to renew humanity. So if all these things are already here so what it will be that different in the age of consciousness?

Here everything for human shall be decided by the consciousness & not by mind's prejudice. By saying so aren't we going to become once again an archaic or primitive society in the age of consciousness? Once we put consciousness at the driving seat the outcome will be spontaneity. But just consider if we move away from self conscious and thinking part of us then action which will spring from consciousness will be altogether spontaneous just like that of a lion, or a cow, or a member of primitive tribe. All of them do not apply 'mind' to whatever they perform.

The hidden part of consciousness may be the driving force for many of our unconscious actions, many of them wrong and uncivil and even the actions that we actually do not want to perform. The consequences of saying good bye to ego are many and some of them you really won't appreciate.

The journey that man has accomplished till today to become civil was to undergo meticulous discipline of becoming self-conscious by development of thoughts, philosophizing the existence and repression of spontaneity which makes him outrageous. Why do some of us suffer more may be because of being more spontaneous and less self conscious.

A murderer merely suffers because of his spontaneity in taking less civil decision. The thinking part of the ego may be causing us to suffer in our mental world yet it curbs our freedom in a way to prohibit our uncivil actions.

So why should we want to turn the wheel back and put consciousness at the center of man's doings? Is really the spontaneity or the lack of it the cause of our sufferings?

But consciousness groups say when we nurture ego we lack spontaneity. We nurture methodological and disciplinary ego. Spontaneity which springs from ego is reactionary and revengeful. It is schematic with hidden motives to get benefit whatever ego perform. It tends to draw benefit even from charitable activities. But spontaneity of consciousness lies in naturalness of behavior which is less methodological and laced with love & kindness. Once subjects become conscious they won't have any ego interference.

Perhaps without becoming so we will utterly fail in our endeavors of becoming members or age of consciousness. Without putting back or cutting down of all the vestiges of egoism we will never achieve that oneness of thoughts which is highest need for our next step to consciousness.

Perhaps these contradictory forces playing with the unconscious in us unreservedly fail us to achieve that shift in consciousness! To go beyond good and bad for some of us is a matter of delight and it is very likely for us to take it in our favor when evil is glorified in such a way and end of relative goodness is forecasted.

While commenting upon such turn of events enlightened ones say, we do not interfere with the ways of nature and we see divine principle in everything. So may we say that we already have everything, all the shades of grey, all the balance of consciousness and ego activity which we need but do not have much enlightenment to appreciate it?

— 0 —

(18)

Religious Stampedes-
A manmade tragedy
(Our Collective Religious Mind)

There arise in mind an endless series of questions provided one is doubtful and receptive to answers!

The questions create questions!

The questions breed questions!!

The questions arise even when we have full mental faculties to answer them.

The questions remain even after we presume to have answered them fully.

The question is not whether the temple, the place of worship exists at a faraway place and had long weary path . . . say on some hilltop or in a desert or watery surroundings or in a busy market or in foreign land and you had much sweat shed before you had the final glimpse of your revered deity.

Or you took a long pilgrimage, with a family of kids, fit and ill both, old and young combined, put yourself to weirdness and vagaries of weather, took a tramp transport and with effort you made the way to worship place among others like you. The question breeds whether you have visited that lone temple that exists in your soul much before this outer temple was built on earth.

The question is not that you decided to undertake the spiritual journey for the sake of spiritual fulfillment that you urgently needed. You wanted to exhaust away the everyday obsession with worldly matters. The question arise whether you knew that you were always on the path of spiritual journey right from the moment you took birth; that your body and spirit are never separate!

The question is not whether you take delight or tension, seeing the long queues before the revered idol or the revered guru and you equate it in the mind the might, the valor, the deity or the guru possess. Or whether you find equal gratification from the discourse of your favorite guru who speaks exotic vocabulary you understand a little and remain consistently busy fanning hot humid air in the open shamiana. The question arise in the event of stampede, the unruly crowd created, the first thing you wanted to save was not your spirit but your body, and in the event of saving that one you destroyed many others who came with the similar motive?

The question is not whether you actually wanted to escape the blaze of hell after death, the moment you decided to undertake the path of spirituality that had a sad end. The answer is that you were actually pushed into the fire of man-made hell.

The question is not that you were unaware of the strength of temporary support on the passage to your beloved deity and it broke down, unable to bear those scores of devotees who decided to visit worship place on the same day. But the question that is not looked into is whether you were aware of the might of your own soul that does not need such ridiculous practices!

The question is not that you were unable to withstand compel of adulation and reverence that you had for the deity. But the next thing to ponder is that you were also unable to resist the pressure of the peer group who is practicing these silly things without any general uplift of society.

(P.S. often witness sad scenes or hear sad news of stampede occurring at religious places. People become an ill-managed crowd when millions of them gather at a particular religious place for the sake of worship. They then put themselves to a grave danger, danger of stampede. Stampedes are recorded in history as manmade tragedy. This is a scriptural wisdom never hidden from dumbest of the dumbest human that the Truth, the reality, the God, the *kripa*, is totally individual effort and individually obtained and you may obtain it sitting at the corner of your own house. The crowd, the collective psyche, the organized worship merely gives hypnotic angle to your quest and end up in more rigorous bondage than your own worldly bondage. The iron in your soul seeks transformation to become steel and be free of all attachments. And not the other way round i.e. to get detached from one magnet of worldly bondage and get attached to another magnet of religious fiefdom.)

(On frequent stampedes[34] at religious places, we witness sadly off and on)

— **0** —

---

[34] **Worst India Stampede:** Over 800 people were killed and 100 injured in a stampede at the Mahakumbh Mela in 1954.

Considering that it was the first Kumbh Fair after the Independence, many leading politicians had visited the city during the event, which goes for over 40 days. What compounded the failure of crowd control measures, over 5 millions pilgrims visit Allahabad during the festival, was not just the presence of large number of politicians.

The fact that the Ganga river had changed course and moved in closer to the Bund (embankment) and the city, further reduced the available space of the temporary Kumbh township and movement of the people.

Source: http://news.rediff.com/slide-show/2010/mar/04/slide-show-1-worst-religious-stampedes.htm#1

(19)

There is no Exterior
to our Existence
(Skin is not the outer limit)

Reality exists as a whole and not as fragmented one appearing as different bodies and separate body parts. What we experience as body the first thing we notice is skin. Does our body end at the skin or start from it? Skin appears as the outermost covering of the body. As in the world we are accustomed to look at the separate bodies, similarly for our body we have tendency to look at different body parts.

To experience reality as a whole behind the veil of separate bodies of the universe would mean to look for the unity at which the separation ends. It would also mean to put an end to the distress of our existence which is separate from the rest. "One who sees the infinite in all things sees God. He who sees the ratio sees himself only, says William Blake[35].

---

[35]   **William Blake (1757-1827)** was an English poet, painter and printmaker. Largely unrecognized during his lifetime, Blake is now considered a seminal figure in the history of the

Beyond the capture of human mind there lies a reality which can be fathomed only by being one with purity of consciousness. This reality is not the reality of mind. This is not reality of senses, of perceptions and of inferences, also not reality of deductions, reasoning and conclusions. This is not reality of knowledge. This is not reality of apparently divisible separable, the colorful, noisy, odorous, tasteful, hot or cold world.

That may also be above the reality of feelings and sensations. That is the reality which is entirely non-sensory in nature. To be the knower of that reality first of all we have to go beyond senses, our outer perceptions.

To get into the above statements within a moment we have to divert our eyes from the scene to the process of seeing and then visualization of the visualizer and reflection of it and becoming a mere witness in the end. Only then at this final state we perceive the union of seer with the scene.

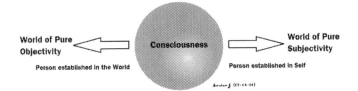

At this state there is union of the universal soul manifest in us with the embodied soul. Within a moment one sees

---

poetry and visual arts of the Romantic Age. His prophetic poetry has been said to form "what is in proportion to its merits the least read body of poetry in the English language". Source: http://en.wikipedia.org/wiki/William_Blake

object uniting with the subject and dissolution of apparent boundary of object & subject. Seer becomes all objects or every other thing becomes subject. Pure self i.e. self without willful ego and the objective world becomes one and there is ever interchanging this way and that way within ever changeable existence.

Consciousness is pure centrality. There is no outer end to it. This means inwardly all things physical and mental, gross and subtle, manifest and non-manifest are contained within the Self, the embodied spirit. Outwardly there is no ending of my body. The seer that is me, the consciousness that is me, the observer that is me is fragmented to millions of eyes of all creatures still this observer retains its single entity.

On the objective side if I start trekking from this pure centrality I cross body of knowledge, then of thoughts and then I cross the body of desires, then comes the body of nervous vibrations and reach the gross vegetative body then enter into environmental body and then enter non-environmental space and finally to totality of universe where I always is. My travelogue will always be in this direction and not the other way round that I start from outer gross body and try to enter my inner self and try to visualize my soul. I will never be able to do that. Here from willful thought I see my gross physical body I enter into nervous vibration field but won't go beyond the thought, the memory & knowledge. I have started with thought and ended up with thought. Thought can reach thought but can't go beyond thought. First of all I have to keep in my mind that I am at the center, the pure consciousness, which is aware of all. Only then all the apparent boundaries dissolve & my travelogue becomes from center to periphery.

That may be our highest state of existence. No knowledge & memory intervene so that is the end of all knowledge. That is the beginning of all knowledge. All methods of curing ailments, all psychotherapies, all motivational blogs, all philosophies are products of this knowledge.

Why to roam at the periphery when you have seen the root. Why to mend a branch when you can mend the whole tree!

Some of us don't want to end at one single witness. if there can be hearer of the hearings, why not extend this process further i.e. hearer of the hearer of hearings or hearer of the hearer of the hearer of the hearings and so on, up to infinity, they say. This is mere theoretic dilemma. This never happens so in practical terms. The consciousness as doer and consciousness as witness exist as a cohesive whole.

At this stage, as we have observed earlier, the consciousness is one with the objects of the world and at the same time one with herself and there is constant shift from objectivity to subjectivity and vice versa even without our particular awareness of this whole swing. We may term this state as that of consciousness at her origin, at pre-reflective state while coming into the world. She has just not tasted, smelled, seen or heard the world!

Once the consciousness is at her state of coming into the world, her rest course will be decided by the choices she first makes in the world. She may decide to live in the world of pure objectivity or in the pure subjectivity. By this simple first choice she will become a worldly or non-worldly doer. She will adopt world or be away from world (become renunciate, sanyasin) later on.

A non-worldly doer creates a space for the subjectivity of consciousness, exist there and remain attached to the universality of consciousness and unattached to the world. A worldly doer remains established in unending worldly affairs.

Some say this is because of our nervous profile i.e. type of brain, nervous system one is born with. While others consider it is because of the original choice consciousness makes at the start of life.

Consciousness living with pure objectivity is well established in the world. Here consciousness makes the choice to be with the world, she merges herself within the objects, with very little attachment to her own subjectivity. Obsessively attached to the over-enthusiastic ego, she remains adherent to world of actions and reactions, cause and effect, hurts and counter hurts.

A non-worldly doer is also not unattached from the world. Here consciousness may turn away from all personal motives in this world. But as an unattached doer he now strives for higher good of the world. We call these persons born with such consciousness as philanthropist and they have very little personal life; they have so much love with humanity that they try to alleviate the ailments of humanity. They never leave active life but their activities are not born of their ego, their personal attachments, hates and love & never for their personal gain. Like Krishna world's best known philanthropist, they drive the chariot of others; help them to achieve their justified goals.

On the other side consciousness living with pure subjectivity, person representing also has nil personal life. Person views every object of the world, living or non-living as the extension of his own self. He sees others from his own subjectivity, as his own subjective self.

Often termed as *sanyasin* he sees the reality behind drama, a single act behind multitude of acts of world affairs. His act of renunciation transcends every major or minor attachment to the self. With overabundant love towards humanity he equally refrains from having any real attachment to beings of his choice. Though he never joins individual pursuits of others but he has great insight for general wellbeing of individuals.

These individuals, philanthropist and the sanyasin are the product of original choice of the consciousness, this way or that way, they are wonderfully free, liberated fellows.

Rest all others, exhibiting many shades of gray, enter into the process of building their worldly ego as their executive personality and forever make so strong bondage with the world and they enter into long term engagement in completing all justified, unjustified goals.

— **0** —

There is no Exterior to our Existence

(20)

All actions happens from
Machine of Nature
(But Man is no Helpless Doer)

W_e always react to something but never act of our own. We react to actions performed by others and also we do carry out our actions and ensuing reactions to endless consequences.

Do we sometime act too with a very original choice? If so what is this original choice. What is this 'free will'?

Does the action performed with an original choice will be devoid of reactions and consequences? No, this is never so as the main component of theory of 'karma' is cause and effect or action and reactions.

Nothing in this world exists without a cause or consequence. Even your 'free act' is also not without a cause. It has some progenitor as a cause and consequence as an effect. There is an endless chain of cause and effect.

Our reactions to other people acts are our unconscious choices. They are perhaps guided by the mental disposition we have. From extreme hostility to extreme love to our immediate surroundings of people and places we have many grades of this mental temperament.

At a given time we have enough stockpile of our past and future actions accomplished or unaccomplished along with their series of consequences on the work table of life. So badly entangled we are in this chain that we may not be able to find that original action whose consequences we are carrying forward.

There was some original action which came to our life long time back. May at the time when we were not aware. We took it up as an unconscious choice. We made it as our unconscious goal. We have just forgotten what it was. But having forgotten that action, we are now enough programmed to respond and carry forward its endless consequences.

These endless consequences have given birth to many more actions. Each action has created its own consequence. Isn't that something horrible part in our life that we are bound to such a long chain of actions and reaction? Had we not been unconscious of performing certain activities or just forgetful to some others, we must have strangulated ourselves with this chain. At physical level we know only one immediate action and one its immediate consequence as and when it unfolds. But at mental level we have many!

Every consequence takes two routes to produce its effect. They are mental and physical route. By physical we mean social or environmental. This effect affects us and our surroundings purely in physical way. Taking mental route action produces a mental or psychological effect upon us and those near to us creates mental consequences. This mental effect is one we must be very careful to own. We are of the habit to ask continuously whether this action of ours was primarily good or bad as per social values. We would then put our action in the category of good or bad. Ensuing social reaction also help us to categorize our actions. You cannot ignore this psychological effect howsoever hardboiled or thick skinned you may be. When immediate social reaction is not available to some of the secret actions of yours, you collect or accumulate the mental consequences which may go beyond even your life time to affect your genetic makeup and perhaps affect the progeny. Medical science has proofs that some actions when go to mental level and affect our thoughts. They start lowering your immunity level and become cause of many incurable ailments like Depression, Hypertension, Heart disease, Diabetes, even Cancer and untreatable Infections.

The physical consequences of our actions affect our individual and social life in both positive and negative manner. Physical consequences affect both our social and professional life and you may raise or drop your social and financial status. These physical effects affect both related and unrelated persons in our life and our immediate and distant kin.

Bound by such chain of actions and reactions in life can we work out some solutions to break this chain?

To understand we must start with a query to ourselves. What is our relationship to nature, the totality of universe, or God if some of you prefer so?

By becoming separate from the nature should our goal of life be to create a separate niche for ourselves, continuously make improvements into it till you become the uncontested ruler of your territory. Should our future goal be to attain a level of moral height where people must adore us, worship us as we worship nature or God or gods and we are categorized in the class of gods even after death. Do some of us want somehow to attain a position where nature & her other creations look upon us as some great being with superior ethical & moral as well as public status. Should we in later life be able to cage and domesticate nature subduing all its harshness and adversity? If not entirely at conscious level but some of us definitely think on these lines.

They no more want to remain servants or puppets of nature but ultimately want to make nature their puppet. Would it ever be possible for a man to become lord of universe, they perhaps unconsciously think? Since ancient times there is no dearth of people who have started from early life with one single goal to become a ruler of whole world with ultimate end to attain uncontested sovereignty of whole universe. If heroes and antiheroes of pulp fiction and cartoon characters are believed to carry secret psychological missions of humanity at large then these assertions do carry some meaning. Man since ancient times has believed that universe is a sort of political establishment where God is the king while whole creation including human population is the subjects. One of man's secret missions is to become good lord himself, perhaps—I may be wrong.

Does this universe stand externally to fulfill my desires and to complete my highest ever secret and obvious ambitions to conquer the precarious nature till she subdues to my whims of being highest ever evolved specie the *Homo sapiens.*

Before we declare further such senseless assertions, let's remind ourselves.

Nature would never create a creation which would surpass her own structure. This would go against universal laws of creation. Nature won't allow her creation to become that strong to annihilate the nature herself.

Yes, nature can be harmed in parts by man or any other specie or by some internal damage but not *in toto.*

Nature is a big machine.

Nature is the functional part of manifest universe. How vast it is.

Actually functional nature is not controlled by some single entity like God but regulated by its own diverse creatures. The biological nature comprising animals and plants co-exist and help each other's existence that we all know. But this coexistence is guided by many facts which we often term as the secret functioning of nature. For example feedback loops guide the functioning of nature in a marvelous way. These are positive feedback loops and negative feedback loops. In simpler terms feedback loops are action-reaction consequence. To maintain regularity and rhythm, nature keeps itself in balance. Whenever there is disturbance which cause imbalance in nature there occur a chain of reactions.

Feedback loops play their part in maintaining balance in situations as big as development of hurricanes in the vast sea or land bodies or as small as anger bursts in a person. Economy boom and depressions too are regulated by feedback loops. These are examples of positive feedback. Negative feedback is seen in price stability or supply demand as well as homeostasis in human body.

All physical, chemical and biological activity in the universe submits to this law of nature. Most of our collective social, financial and political life is rather dependent on these regulatory laws of nature. Man being certainly higher specie is as much the slave of nature as slave of his own whims. So what is a simple law of nature to keep balance everywhere man would turn the tables to his side and would see cruelty in natural laws? So man as a product of nature would use all his physico-mental efforts to fight back and conquer its cruelty.

He would challenge natural laws to transport resources to survive in hardest ever deserts. There is forever struggle between harshest conditions of nature and survival of specie. But nature has its own diverse ways and would never open up all her secrets. Even if nature's secrets are well understood they would never let down the specie, its own creation be they the men or any other. Nature's laws would even destroy a part of creation for the benefit of creation at large.

Man with his limited vision considers that he will somehow someday will conquer nature and become the master of universe.

This earth is visited upon by great men of wisdom, the saints, the prophets and they all when talking about man's relation with nature have always affirmed that man is a servant of nature or God meaning totality is the master nature.

Man by his doings considers he is doing for himself. Nature by her doings actually does for whole of creation man included.

So nature is supreme doer. Man is an individual doer. Like all other creatures does all doings to fill his belly. Mental part of his nature somehow creates desires and he starts overdoing his doings. But overall man just brings about actions which are inevitably guided and dictated by supreme nature.

He does all his doings for the nature.

Nature does her doings through man.

But somehow with limited vision and limited understanding and under influence of ego he falsely considers that he is the doer.

There is no separation in man and nature. Man and nature are not dual pair. They are one. They are non-dual.

Driving in hilly areas at night is a real illusion. You want to reach the city next and you judge by lights glittering on the next mountain that your destination is quite near. Time and again it seems that you are just there. But by the time you've taken the next turn, lights disappear only to appear again after subsequent turn. You are there but you are not.

This is how it happens in one's natural state and learned state.

In natural state one is always there where in learned state one presumes himself to be only to learn in the next moment that he is not there.

Action is universal comprizing a long chain Action given to next after performance by one player

Prime 'Doer' of all actions is Nature

ACTION

Swaran J. (02-04-14)

Action performed in the dual mode is the action performed by a thought. This is action performed by first willing it. Making will and then performing action is a dual-action. One who makes will for action first will definitely take responsibility for his action.

One who creates action-less state for himself would be left out of all responsibilities. This action-less sate is a state of spontaneity. This is making all actions unwilled, unplanned, non-passionate, spontaneous, and non-methodological. The person goes in *sahaj-bhaav* state and never bothers what action comes out from him. If we understand nature deeply the same features are there in all actions of nature.

All actions start from nature. In many religious philosophies nature is said to be prime doer. Karta Purkh. There is continuity of action from nature up to you. A person wrongly believing that he is performing an action for his own sake is actually doing duty as a faithful subject of nature.

When you perform an action for sake of nature you are acting on behalf of nature. All your actions begin primarily from nature, even the passionate ones for example a person making love to a woman is actually doing nature's job to expand and procreate. While performing for nature you put yourself in inaction mode.

In inaction you become merely an action, neither performer nor the end result seeker. You are a conduit. Action comes from somewhere; you are a part player and then action transferred to next player. This is Vishavkarma; whole of the universe in activity.

One who has not entirely submitted his will or ego to perform action is in dual mode. One has not freed himself from the chain of action reaction sequence.

To transcend the willing part which is the first step of inaction one is to transcend the ego part, the thought of action.

When a man regards the action as if it were for him, he has 'action-mentality', and when he treats his action as God-ordained and for God, he being just a silent doer, an action-less doer or mere doer tool. He has then 'inaction-mentality'.

But once learned all these parameters of inaction does it mean that we have come to the natural state of performance.

In animals there is only spontaneous will. They perform an action to fulfill body needs but don't get frustrated if they fail. Their ego is less developed.

Man performs actions methodically after proper weighing and calculations. He does not want to fail. He has already weighed the outcome or fruit of the action in his mind and thoughts.

Non-duality of action ends in spontaneity. During spontaneous performance you have not given time to ego to raise its head. You have not weighed the performance and also not the end results. You have also not given enough time to the thought of subsequent action. You are in a mind free state. To be mind and ego free creates spontaneity in man. Reaction is the spontaneity in animals.

Here you act without giving thought but not without awareness. You act with deeper love for action. You act with deeper love for the humanity. Once involved in thought you have become methodological. You have permitted entry of mind and ego through the thought activity. They start guiding the action making it ego centered action.

But such state of affair when merely learned from Shastra or from Gurus and guides create next form of duality. Thought is still there. Like:

"Oh! Shastra don't say this. Guru doesn't prescribe this. I must do this. I must not do that . . . ."

Even such state of action makes the action planned and methodological. Making it ego centered. Here ego striving hard to establish as pious person.

At one stage of life you perform a learned non-duality. But you go completely dual by performing willful and thought out actions in the stage next.

You have to be free from the learned guidance from books and guides. Once free from the learned guidance if you are still in dual thoughtful mode again your doer is not vanished yet. Now there may be a better option. Better than to wear learned non-duality or non-action or inaction. Better to be a complete natural. Better to be a natural egoistic mode than to be a learned hypocrite non-doer. At some stage your performing ego will be dropped naturally.

We are conscious beings.

We are free beings. The consciousness in us is condemned to be free. We have a temporal worldly creator in form of our immediate parents. We have divine creator as nature who creates us for her own mysterious reasons.

We live to live. We live to sustain life in us. The whole legal system binds us to a collective way of life and allows or disallows us for certain actions to perform. It is there to only put "civic chains" only to our doings. This is merely an arrangement by us humans, to maintain sanctity and integrity of society. society creates a minor or major control on our personal freedom. This is the **"worldly law"**.

But we are governed by "divine law" too. This is the same law of nature which works in totality. This law keeps balance. It is not passionate. As we submit to the worldly law ordained by society for greater benefit of the society we must submit to the 'divine law' too for the greater benefit to Mother Nature.

The values on which our social and legal system is based change with changing times.

So this can be never said with utmost certainty that a particular doing is "Sinful" or "virtuous", was so in the past and will not remain same in the future. In ancient time's performance of violent actions, to do killings were considered to be "virtuous" ones. Time and again Lord Krishna advises Arjuna in Gita to fight and kill his kin as a divine duty to establish a rule of order. Now these days you would never say with utmost sincerity that you are performing an action of killing someone for promotion of *Dharma* or Virtue in the society. But every person may have his or her own sense of dharma so with changing times we have different set of values and different sort of legal and social binding to judge our actions.

Otherwise we are free to perform any activity on earth. We are also free to take our own life in extreme circumstances. But this freedom of ours just evaporates when we confront consequence of our actions. After experiencing the negative consequence of our one particular action we are forever forbidden to perform that action again. Nothing, not even any spiritual, non-spiritual philosophy hits our head the way a negative experience can.

But the question is does these consequences remain up to our life time or travel beyond than that. What is the deep cause of "sense of sin or virtue" in us?

All actions happens from Machine of Nature

So why do we put our actions in "virtuous" of "sinful" category. Why is there that great moral binding on us humans? While plants and animals are free from such bindings. A particular action may become virtuous in one setting and become totally sinful in another one. Example— you steal to feed a person dying with starvation or you kill a wrong doer who is going to outrage modesty of a woman.

The question to decide is whether "sin" is caused by performing one particular action. May this action be "murder" or "stealing" or simply an act of "lying" etc. What actually amount to sin? Do we really turn sinful by simply acting on a momentary decision of us and which at that time appeared totally valid? Why do we repent on the actions performed in past whereby at the time of performance we never had such (negative) feeling?

This whole action drama is merely subjective experience because it actually gives me insight into my whole life while I seriously examine my own action-reaction consequences. All acts termed sinful are negative ones because they put an unpleasant feeling in me after performance. My own subjective reactions forbid me for doing such action in future. I even would advise my children to remain away from such actions. If I am a teacher in a bigger area then I would advise a large number of people to avoid such action. Such an over expression of these feelings in society at large create a bias (you can say positive bias) towards all our negative acts.

This makes me as a player in the world of actions as well as an observer to understand and realize my own reactions and recognize and discriminate my prejudicial and non-prejudicial responses.

This create in me a good observer who can judge my responses and their long term results and curb my reaction there and then if I find them to be totally unworthy of performance.

This also makes me aware of the long chain of action reaction consequence which necessarily forbids me to be too much indulgent in unnecessary actions.

This also makes me understand of unnecessary ego indulgence and create a non-passionate me out of my passionate performances.

This gives me somewhat a vague sense of an action-less action which I sense as a right option but very difficult to perform.

This unquestionably divides my actions as personal and collective. The collective actions are when I act in a big field alongside many performers in social or governmental institutions. Here I have a shared responsibility of actions.

This also shows me a way where I can simply get out from the karmic chain by doing social and collective actions only without becoming a total renunciate (sanyasin) of actions.

This also makes me aware that it is not the external work done by me as important. Important is the internal work that my psyche does while performance of action.

This also gives me the understanding of that supreme verse of Gita where I can understand that result or fruit of action is not in my hand. Then I just altogether become a non-performer, not disinterested in action but carrying actions as the individual and collective responsibility. I have given hands and feet so I am required by the supreme nature to act. I act because I have been provided tools of actions— mind, intellect and body.

P.S.-To summarize: To comprehend result of an action, an action comes up with two consequences

1) Action brings result

2) Action brings fruit

The first kind is action reaction type physical consequence causing change in our individual life as well as in others for whom action has been primarily performed. It does cause change in many others who are in vicinity but not the immediate recipient. The consequences never end but keep on multiplying as per

The second kind are the mental consequences based on what one personally gains by performing an action

Praise or condemnation

Sin or Virtue

Good or bad feeling

Revengeful or Do good type mentality

These fruits are unnecessarily attached

We have created and nurtured them since ages.

These are traps of karma.

These bind us to next sequence of action. They compel us to follow the reaction. They create in us the sort of human animal—compulsive and reactionary.

For this it has been said

If I do not accept praise for myself condemnation will also not be mine.

— 0 —

All actions happens from Machine of Nature

Epilogue-I

Beyond the Object
(Beyond Human Body and towards Body Human!)

The object is what is seen before our eyes while the subject is right with in. What lies beyond the object?

The subject being the observer within! Observing, interpreting and understanding! Building up the memory and knowledge for collecting the observations for future use! With time it collects so many observations and interpretations that it loses the capacity for further observation. Stale interpretations end up with the biased understanding. Dullness strikes and intellect gets strained enough to look at the world without presupposed and accepted view. It loses the capacity of fair observation. It observes those objects which are ripe for its immediate understanding. Unripe and fresh remain beyond understanding. It loses contact with the innovative world as it loses creative thinking. How to comprehend what is beyond the object when fatigued intellect had not completely figured out object?

We interpret the object from its past history and future possibilities, its antecedents and descendants. But object is simply not what we see and interpret. Object is not what we understand. Object is beyond our limited interpretation. Object is beyond our premeditated knowledge and belief.

Object stands alone. Beyond the object is the reality of the object. Beyond the object we may find the true elucidation of the object.

Beyond the object lies the field of imagination and creativity. Nature conceived man as conscious subject. Perhaps that is why we are supposed to be imaginative and creative. Always having astonishing novelty of thoughts! Always bubbling with fresh ideas!

Is the act of creation an act of will? The process of creation is an act of non-doing, a sort of unconscious doing, a doing without any deliberate 'will to do'. With 'will' we accomplish, without 'will' we create!

The virtue of non-doing is creating something before the 'will to create' spoils the creation.

The will to create is not the creation. It is simply a construction that we accomplish with our learnt abilities. It is planned activity. We suppose first and create then. To call construction the creation becomes our life long obsession. We redo and polish! This learned creation is worldly, planned and premeditated and never divine.

The learned creation as we understand in the world today has always been an act of copying in the same capacity as our progenitor monkeys. Just keeping count of the established ideas of norms and behavior and reshuffling them to put forward as new creation would not be called so! True creation is putting aside this learned capability and intellect and looking at the object as an intense onlooker, as a non-passionate observer.

The original creation would be the interplay of some primordial intellect, some semi-conscious body movements and some involuntary nervous reflexes. While one creates one becomes tool of creation just like brush and pen, mouse and keyboard! Away from being a willful creator, one becomes an act, simply an act of creation. Person becomes the act! The act of creation just happens, brought about by primordial nature working within. Creator come to know only after the creation is finally before his eyes.

Man is always beyond his vegetative body; man is beyond his biological object. Individual man supposes a person in his physical body and for lifelong remains occupied with it. He never knows he may be more than mere psyche, more than his wishes and desires, more than his wills and performances. He is beyond that. Beyond the man is one who is creative and imaginative. Beyond the man is the pure observer. Beyond the man is nature, the prime doer and prime being.

What is the human body and what is the body human? Human body and body human are not separate things. What a man does for himself the body human does for humanity. It is the care. It is the concern. A single human cares for his body, his personal territory. Body human cares for territory of all humans. Body human is conglomerate of many humans. Individual man struggles to exist; body human treads the path of struggle for all humans with the caravan of time.

The body human may be an assembly of few men and women who understand and look beyond themselves or it may be the body of scores of individuals. The caravan of humanity is cavalcade of men who have gone beyond their individualistic desires and mundane concerns and have started funding the collective needs of mankind.

Individual intellect is not the product of the individual brain. It is the product of collective struggle of whole of mankind. Individual brain invents for itself a psychological refuge, an individual psyche, an ego, an executive to deal with the world. Similarly body human harbors a collective psyche. Collective psyche of ours is similarly creative and imaginative as the individual man.

Going beyond human body may be like going beyond the humanistic tendencies and experiencing the wonder of wonders—the individual human consciousness getting its refined merger into the co-consciousness of the mankind!

Caravan of humanity looks beyond the object! Beyond the individual bodies; beyond the individual needs! It looks beyond the accepted norms. It discovers the principals of collective living; discovers the laws which bind humanity closely with nature. It does not invent the pre-meditated laws; it does not do some group planning for subjugating the fare needs of humanity. It does not put lid over the needful aspirations of humanity. It rather finds solace in applying principals of nature to individual and collective psyche.

Caravan of humanity harbors wishes to let life to flow like an unsullied river and does not desire anyway to breed life in a stagnant pool.

The caravan of humanity breaks the old stale value system of society and refreshes it with the eternal and primeval values. Humans with meager intellect and understanding take pride in breaking rules for selfish motives. But caravan of humanity breaks them for the collective good.

Individually the associates of body human may not possess the super-human intellect but collectively they employ the minimum of intellect but abundant motivational force to look at the imperfections in the existing morals.

The eternal human values remain covered under the grime of ritual and rites of the pre-historic era. Habitual biases of the tired brains of society fail to uncover them. This is not the high intellectuals but audacious amongst men who dust away the rituals and find the fine radiance of the original human values. Finding elemental values is just but going beyond the individual and putting the human behavior in context of nature.

Fundamental human value that the body human campaigns, is submission to nature. Submission to nature is not to become a perfunctory puppet in her hands. Not to become slave to lusty and violent nature within. Submission to nature is to put nature as prime planner and keeping individual aspirations at bay. It is to regain the original human freedom of primordial man who was always free of thinking brain.

It tends to regain the choice of activity. We have lost this primary choice to the manipulative mind which merely extends its past to the future. It extends its aspirations to ambitions.

Present mind has created a restricted worldly order of rules and regulations. Once in the bondage it cries for freedom! Such rules certainly are not delivered by nature. This worldly order is motivated by selfish needs of society; divided into haves and have-nots; to cause human split into working and disciplining class.

Few men who control do not ride the cavalcade of humanity. They are the mere territorial guardians to keep the human mind and body in the irons of established norms.

Body human wishes for humanity to be the subject of nature where joint and personal territory is cherished with equal passion, where live and let live is the fundamental value. It is not for making humanity to be the protracted succession of controllers and oppressors, all riding a ladder, one controlling the next.

Those who submit to principals of nature and ask others to do so are the caravan of humanity which till today have tread thorny paths and will continue to do so till oneness is achieved at every level of human existence.

— **0** —

Epilogue-II

Those humans with infantile souls

I wish their soul grow and bloom

Those humans who have spent hopes of life

I wish they look beyond self imposed gloom

Those humans caged in rigid thought

I wish they find in them a natural clown

The humans who have become cultural slaves

I wish they reinstate as an indigenous commune!!!

(P.S.—Can we? Can we establish ourselves one day as an indigenous commune i.e. commune of humanity comprising whole world? Can we some day in fine morning, speak from heart:

"O' sweet nature! Your secrets are great. We no more want to 'think and act'. We now want to 'obey and act'!"

Now the beginning:

With this ends the ABC of the Inner World, my small effort to communicate the some of the basic realities of our inner world. But that is not the end! Now onus is on the reader to continue with the rest of alphabets . . . .

The end